THE POCKET GUIDE TO
FOSSILS

Kingdoms	Animal types	Large divisions (including phyla)	Sub-phyla (or similar)	Classes	Sub-classes	Number of genera
PLANTS		ALGAE				3
		OTHER PLANTS				14
ANIMALS	**INVERTEBRATES**	BRYOZOA				1
		PROTOZOA				1
		CNIDARIA		ANTHOZOA		14
		PORIFERA				5
		ECHINODERMATA		CRINOIDEA		6
				ECHINOIDEA		16
				ASTEROIDEA		3
		BRACHIOPODA				25
		HEMICHORDATA		GRAPTOLITHINA		5
		ARTHROPODA	TRILOBITA			29
			OTHER ARTHROPODS			9
		MOLLUSCA		SCAPHOPODA		1
				BIVALVIA		30
				GASTROPODA		26
				CEPHALOPODA	NAUTILOIDEA	6
					AMMONOIDEA	47
					COLEOIDEA	3
	VERTEBRATES	TRACE FOSSILS				9
		FISH				14
		AMPHIBIANS				1
		REPTILES				3
		MAMMALS				1
		FOSSIL TEETH				11

This chart is not intended to be a classification of organisms, but is designed to help the reader understand the organization of this book; the headings in the book follow this general scheme. In most cases, this follows biological and palaeontological practice, but some other sub-divisions are also used. The great majority of the names for the individual fossils are at generic level.

THE POCKET GUIDE TO
FOSSILS

CHRIS M. PELLANT

PARKGATE
BOOKS

First published in 1992

This edition published in 1997 by
Parkgate Books Ltd
London House
Great Eastern Wharf
Parkgate Road
London SW11 4NQ
Great Britain

9 8 7 6 5 4 3 2 1

British Library Cataloguing in Publication Data
The catalogue record for this book is available from the British
Library.

ISBN 1 85585 360 4

Editor Patricia Burgess
Designer Ian Youngs
Art Director Dave Allen
Editorial Director Pippa Rubinstein

Printed in Italy

Contents

Geological Time Scale

PERIODS		ERAS	EONS
RECENT	QUATERNARY	CAENZOIC	PHANERZOIC
PLEISTOCENE			
PLIOCENE	TERTIARY		
MIOCENE			
OLIGOCENE			
EOCENE			
PALAEOCENE			
CRETACEOUS		MESOZOIC	
JURASSIC			
TRIASSIC			
PERMIAN		UPPER PALAEOZOIC	
CARBONIFEROUS			
DEVONIAN			
SILURIAN		LOWER PALAEOZOIC	
ORDOVICIAN			
CAMBRIAN			
		PRE-CAMBRIAN	PROTEROZOIC
			ARCHAEAN

Left scale (millions of years): 0.01, 2, 5, 22.5, 37.5, 53.5, 65, 136, 190, 225, 280, 345, 395, 440, 500, 600, 4600

Right scale (millions of years): 600, 2500, 4600

NB The base of each division is in millions of years from the present

Introduction

Fossils are defined as any record of past life, the word 'fossil' meaning something that has been dug up. This definition covers many types of material, and the great diversity of fossils is shown in this book. As well as preserved shells and bones, the definition includes unaltered organic material, such as skin and tissue, and also the footprints, tracks, trails and excrement left to tell us that an animal has existed. Geologists tend to regard fossils and their study (palaeontology) as a science that does not include human remains and artefacts. These are the province of the archaeologist, although there is considerable overlap when dealing with the more ancient hominids.

It is very important to regard fossils as the natural history of the past. There is an outcry when rare wild flowers or animals are collected or persecuted, but when great quantities of fossils are collected for sale and monetary gain, such as the *Calymene* trilobites from Morocco, nothing is said or done to prevent it. The problem with this trade in fossils is that the specimens are lost to science, and as they are rarely named or located, they become merely objects of curiosity.

Identification of fossils will not always be possible and expert help may be needed. Having a locality will aid this identification, and gives the specimen scientific value. Even amateurs often make important discoveries.

As they are biological remains, fossils are named using rules of biological nomenclature. This uses Latin names, a sensible system started by the Swedish naturalist Carolus Linnaeus, as long ago as 1735. He chose Latin as the universal standard because there were already English, German, French, Dutch and other local names for many organisms. Take the Jurassic ammonite *Parkinsonia parkinsoni*, for example. The first Latin word is the generic name and the second is the specific name.

How fossils form

Only a very small number of the countless organisms that have existed become fossilized. One of the fascinations and frustrations of palaeontology is that we can only guess at what a whole ecosystem at a given time in the past might have been like. For example, when we discover an entire range of advanced organisms fossilized together and representing a community of animals and plants, that environment must also have supported other animals and plants that are not preserved as fossils. The reason for this incompleteness lies in the ways in which fossils are preserved, but there are more than enough fossils to keep scientists occupied for many years yet!

In order for a shell, bone, tooth, plant stem or footprint to

Here a large ammonite has been preserved as a crushed shell and impression on a shale bedding plane. The cliffs in the background and the rocks on the boulder-strewn, wave-cut platform are of Lower Jurassic age and contain many fossils, including other ammonites, bivalve molluscs, and occasional marine vertebrates. Fossils such as this large, crushed ammonite are impossible to collect, and a camera is the best way of recording them.

be preserved, it must be in equilibrium with its new surroundings when buried in layers of rock. This environment is very different from that in which an organism lived. It helps if the organism has some hard parts, such as a shell, which will survive the rigours of time after its death before burial in sediment takes place, to protect and possibly preserve it. Since much sediment is deposited in the sea, and the land surface is the zone of weathering and erosion, fossils of marine creatures predominate in the fossil record.

To maintain the equilibrium, or balance, that has been mentioned, a shell, for example, buried in sea-bed mud, may be replaced with new minerals and therefore changed chemically. This process, in which fluids carrying minerals in solution impregnate the shell and change it, is called 'petrifaction'. Fossils are commonly replaced with pyrite or silica. These same fluids can often remove the shell or bone to leave a hollow in the strata, which may, at a later date, be infilled with minerals, or with sediment, and a fossil cast formed from the mould. Carbon in plants, fish and even reptiles is often the only surviving material after the organism has been buried in sediment for some time. Fossils of plants, for example, often consist only of delicate carbon films.

Instead of being changed chemically, fossils can retain their original composition. Becoming a fossil does not necessarily imply being changed to stone. Insects are often preserved in amber, which was once sticky, fragrant resin on a pine tree; mammals are caught in peat and tar swamps, and preserved intact; mammoths are deep-frozen in tundra ice.

Some of the most amazing fossils are delicate organisms, such as dragonflies and soft-bodied creatures, preserved by a fluke of geology. A famous case is that of the Burgess Shales in British Columbia. Here, because of a submarine fall of very fine sediment, an assemblage of unique soft-bodied worms,

This ammonite shell has been replaced, and to some extent infilled with quartz crystals. These have taken the place of the original aragonite of which the living shell was made.

Insects can become trapped in the sticky resin that oozes from pine trees. This hardens to amber and fossilizes the entire insect.

jellyfish and other creatures has been preserved. The great importance of this deposit is that it gives us an insight into what were probably typical Cambrian sea-bed life forms, in addition to those such as trilobites, which were commonly fossilized because of their hard shells.

As well as the creatures themselves, their tracks, trails, eggs and excrement provide trace fossils, which can be of great significance. Some organisms are known only from such traces and we can but estimate their size and shape.

Stratigraphic uses of fossils

Stratigraphy is the science concerned with organizing the various strata in the Earth's crust into the correct sequence, and suggesting what environments existed in the past in different parts of the world. One of the main values of fossils is that they help stratigraphers to date rocks relatively and to correlate them over considerable distances. A pioneer of the stratigraphic use of fossils was the English canal engineer William Smith (1769-1839). He had ready access to freshly cut sections through southern England, and was quick to realize that certain fossils were representative of certain strata. He identified these rock beds by their contained fossils, and correlated them over many miles. The basic principles he established are still used.

Plant tissue can be replaced and fossilized by a variety of minerals, one of which is opal, seen here. The tree's growth rings and some detail of the vascular tissue are visible.

This brachiopod shell has been replaced by pyrite, none of the original calcareous structure remaining, but the ribs and other detail on the shell are preserved.

Here, numerous small bivalve molluscs have been infilled with fine-grained sediment, then the rock has been weathered to show cross-sections of the shells.

Though some fossil genera survived for very long periods of time, many are found in relatively short vertical thicknesses of strata, and therefore probably lasted for only a short period of time. These are the fossils of value in stratigraphic work. It is also useful in correlation if the fossil has a wide geographic range, so free-swimming marine creatures are ideal. By using fossils in this way a precise relative time-scale has been built up. The smallest manageable time unit is the zone, defined by the occurrence of a particular fossil species in the strata. Each zone is named after the representative fossil; for example, the first time zone in the Jurassic period is named after the ammonite *Psiloceras planorbis*. A number of zones make a period, and periods are grouped into eras. When the results of radiometric dating are added to the scale it is seen that zones

Psiloceras planorbis
This ammonite, which is typically crushed on shale bedding planes, is the zone fossil for the lowest ammonite zone in the Jurassic. This period, which lasted 54 million years, has over 60 ammonite zones, each on average representing about 850,000 years.

Didymograptus
Graptolites are widespread fossils, possibly because they were planktonic. Species of this 'tuning-fork' graptolite genus are used as zone fossils for four of the zones in the Ordovician period.

may represent less than one million years – a tiny part of geological time. The time-scale here has been established by using fossils and other stratigraphic techniques. Radiometric dating gives the absolute, numerical ages of the subdivisions.

The rocks in which fossils appear
There are three main groups of rocks: igneous, metamorphic and sedimentary. The first is the result of the cooling of molten rock, such as lava; the second group forms as a result of heat and pressure acting on preformed rocks; the third group is made from mud, clay, sand, pebbles and other material deposited on the sea-bed, in lakes and rivers, and on the land. It is sedimentary rocks that most often contain fossils.

There are three categories of sediments, all of which can be fossiliferous. The detrital, or fragmentary, sediments are made of sand, pebbles, mud and other grains worn off pre-existing rocks by the processes of weathering and erosion. These grains are then carried by rivers, glaciers, the wind and ocean currents to be deposited in layers. Most of these rocks are formed in the sea and other environments teeming with life, so fossils are common in rocks such as clay, mudstone, shale and sandstone.

Micraster cortestudinarium
This echinoid, preserved here in brown flint, is a zone fossil for part of the Upper Cretaceous. This type of creature does not fulfil many of the criteria which most zone fossils meet, as it was a burrower into the soft lime mud on the sea bed, which in time became chalk.

Paradoxides
Trilobites are zone fossils for part of the Cambrian period. A number of species of this genus are used in the Middle Cambrian. The specimen shown here lacks its long genal spines.

Another group of sedimentary rocks, the organic sediments, are constructed mainly of fossil material. There are many limestones in this group, for example shelly limestone and crinoidal limestone. Coal, made from the remains of plants, is also classified here.

The chemically formed sediments are the final group. As

Shelly limestone
This is a general term for an organic limestone rich in fossils, which may include some shelled creatures. Here there are brachiopod shells, crinoid stem fragments and many elongated bryozoans.

Stratified sedimentary rocks
This magnificent sea-cliff exposure shows one of the main features of sedimentary rocks – stratification. There are alternating layers of shale and limestone, the more resistant limestone standing out as thin, paler layers.

well as containing rocks like potash ore and rock salt, which have no fossils in them, this group contains some limestones, including fossiliferous oolitic limestone.

Sedimentary rocks are best distinguished from igneous and metamorphic rocks by their stratification, or bedding, which represents the original layers in which the grains of sediment were deposited. The presence of fossils is also a good clue. It is possible, however, for some slightly metamorphosed rocks, like slate, to contain fossils, and ash and dust blown from a volcano may settle in the sea to preserve the remains of organisms.

How to look for and find fossils

A fossil-hunting expedition has three essential stages. The first of these is research in books, maps and journals, which will give clues about where to search. Geological maps are an essential part of this groundwork. These show the rock types that occur on the surface, though care has to be taken because fossiliferous strata may be obscured by layers of river alluvium, glacial clays and peat. Once a particular fossil-bearing stratum has been selected on the map, it will be necessary to find exposures of the rock. Guide books are invaluable here, as they should list locations and give accurate map references.

Otherwise, places where rivers and streams cut through the stratum, or where sea cliffs and inland cliffs provide exposures will have to be found. Many good exposures are man-made. These include road and rail cuttings and quarries. It is very

Limestone cliff and scree slope
This inland cliff is a suitable site for fossil collecting. The scree at the base of the cliff, forming a less steep slope, is a good place to search, and the broken blocks may provide fine material. Corals, brachiopods and molluscs may be found at such sites.

important to remember that all land is owned by individuals or organizations, and that any rock and fossil specimens are in fact the landowner's property. Permission must always be sought before going on to land and collecting material.

The second stage is to go into the field. It is important to take plenty of collecting bags and protective material, such as bubble-wrap, in which to pack any specimens found. Collect in moderation, and resist the use of a geological hammer. This should be used only for breaking up loose blocks, and not for digging away at the exposure. A camera is very useful for recording details of the location and the fossils it provides, and notes should be made of the strata and fossils collected.

Finally comes the curating stage, once the collected specimens have been brought home. Many will need further treatment, such as cleaning and the removal of rock debris. This can be done with a variety of tools, ranging from fine paint brushes to a knife blade or bradawl. When prepared, the specimens should be carefully stored, preferably in small, individual card trays, with a location and name label. These trays will fit into the drawers of a filing cabinet, the metal type being inexpensive and ideal for storing most material.

Waterfall
Here a small river has cut an impressive waterfall and steep-sided gorge. The fallen blocks contain molluscs and other fossils. These are ideal for easy collecting.

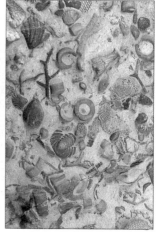

Limestone fossils
This mass of fossils, including trilobites, brachiopods, crinoids and corals, was found as a small rock fragment on a scree slope.

Plants

Some of the earliest fossils are those of algal mounds called Stromatolites, which occur in rocks of Pre-Cambrian age and may be as old as 3,500 million years. They were among the first organisms to produce oxygen. Ever since then plants have been releasing this gas into the atmosphere and thus ensuring the survival of the many organisms that depend on oxygen for their existence. Fossil Stromatolites are found in many areas, and live today in Australia. Some of the earliest stemmed plants are found in rocks of Silurian age, over 3,000 million years younger than the Pre-Cambrian algae. Plants are found in greater abundance and variety in rocks of the Devonian and Carboniferous periods. The latter system contains the world's major coal reserves, which are derived from plant tissue. It was only towards the end of the Jurassic period that plants began to develop flowers. Indeed, the evolution of plants is intimately associated with the development of other forms of life. Only after plants had released abundant oxygen could large oxygen-using animals develop, and insects evolve that fed on the sugars in plant nectar and pollen.

Parka

This fossil of an algal plant shows the circular structure of the thallus with numerous smaller, rounded internal parts. The plant produced spores covered with resistant cuticle, and may have been one of the first to become adapted to living with at least some of its structure above the water surface.
Size The specimen illustrated is about 30mm (1.2in) in diameter.

Distribution *Parka* is a primitive plant from rocks of Silurian and Devonian age. The specimen shown is from the Devonian of Angus, Scotland.

Cooksonia

This important fossil is the first vascular plant (a plant with veins) to be found in the fossil record. The slender stems, which carry spore capsules, contain xylem channels for transporting fluids. These plants lived in swampy environments. *Cooksonia* is classified with the group called Psilophytes.

Size The whole specimen shown here is about 70mm (2.8in) across.

Distribution *Cooksonia* is found in rocks of Silurian and Devonian age in North America, Europe, Africa, Asia and Antarctica. The fossil, a type specimen, is from the Scottish Devonian rocks of Angus.

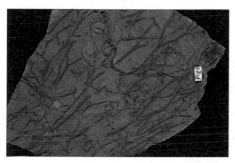

Alethopteris

A delicate fossil, formed as a carbon film on a shale bedding plane. All the original plant tissue has been lost, apart from its carbon. It belongs to the group of plants called Pteridosperms (seed ferns). Such leaves are not uncommon fossils in Upper Palaeozoic strata.

Size The specimen illustrated is about 80mm (3.2in) long.

Distribution A genus from the Carboniferous rocks of North America and Europe.

Lepidodendron

These fossils are of the common Lycopod (clubmoss), which flourished during the Carboniferous period. It was a giant plant, and the various parts of it have been given different biological names because they are found fossilized separately. The roots, for example, are called *Stigmaria*, and the leaves *Sigillaria*. These roots grew nearly horizontally, and the thick stem, part of which is shown in detail here, had a non-woody outer layer with numerous diamond-shaped scars marking the places from which the leaves have broken off. The other specimen is of a leafy branch.

Size The mature plant could reach up to 30 metres (97.5ft) in height.
Distribution This genus is well known in Upper Carboniferous sediments in Europe, north Africa and Asia, including China and Mongolia. It lived in the swampy conditions in which the coal-bearing strata were formed.

Eupecopteris

This fine specimen is preserved inside an ironstone nodule. The delicate leaf structure of this typical Pteridosperm can be seen here, with a single straight axis and many ovoid leaflets.

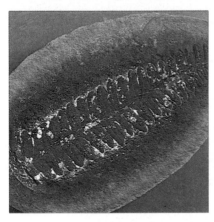

Size The fossil is about 60mm (2.4in) long.
Distribution *Eupecopteris* is known from Upper Carboniferous rocks in Europe, North America and Asia. The specimen shown is from Illinois, USA.

Sphenopteris

As there is little evidence of this plant, apart from its delicate leaves, it is difficult to classify it accurately. The generic name given covers both ferns and seed-ferns. The main feature of this genus is that the leaves have slightly toothed margins.
Size The specimen shown is typical at 60mm (2.4in) in length.
Distribution *Sphenopteris* occurs worldwide in rocks of Carboniferous and Permian age.

Mariopteris

This genus belongs to the Pteridophytes, which are the true ferns. These plants reproduce by spores, and they have to live in a damp environment as water is needed for fertilization. The leaves have a typical central axis and offset leaflets.

Size The specimen illustrated is 55mm (2.2in) long.
Distribution *Mariopteris* is found in Carboniferous rocks in North America and Europe.

Calamites

This is part of the stem of a large horsetail plant, which is typically jointed and also has thin longitudinal markings. The specimen has been preserved by infilling of the hollow stem with sand, which is now sandstone containing small, glittering flakes of mica. There is also a thin film of black carbon on the surface of the fossil, which is all that remains of the original tissue of the plant stem.
Size The section shown is about 120mm (4.8in) long. Mature plants reached 20 metres (65ft) in height.
Distribution *Calamites* is found in rocks of Carboniferous and Permian age in North America, Europe, the CIS, China and Korea.

Neuropteris

This genus of extinct Pteridosperms has leaflets growing from a central stem, which are often oval in shape, and can have smooth edges. In fossils, such leaflets are frequently found separated from the stem. *Neuropteris* was a common plant in the delta swamps of Upper Carboniferous times. These were the swamps where the peat accumulated from which our vast reserves of coal developed. This genus is found with other plant fossils such as *Alethopteris* and *Mariopteris*, all commonly preserved as dark carbonaceous impressions on the surfaces of bedding planes, the original plant material having been lost apart from its essential carbon. Two specimens are illustrated. One is a carbon film and the other is preserved in an ironstone nodule from the famous Francis Creek shale of Illinois, USA.

Size *Neuropteris* leaves are usually about 50mm (2in) in length.

Distribution This genus occurs in rocks of Upper Carboniferous age, in North America and Europe.

Glossopteris

This genus is one of bushy plants belonging to the
Pteridosperm group. A number of leaves have been flattened
on the bedding plane shown in the photograph. They are
characterized by thin veins which curve delicately out from the
central axis of the leaf. *Glossopteris* is of considerable geological
significance because it is found fossilized in rocks in many
landmasses, which indicates that these now separate
continents were once joined together.

Size The mature plant reached about 6 metres (19.5ft)
in height.

Distribution *Glossopteris* is found in the areas that used to
form the supercontinent of Gondwanaland. These are South

America, Australia,
India, Antarctica and
South Africa. The
fossil is of Permian
and Triassic age.
This specimen is
from Adamstown in
Australia.

Ginkgo

A single species of this genus lives today in China and can be
found as a garden plant in many parts of the world. It is a
Gymnosperm and is deciduous. It reproduces sexually, and
there are separate male and female plants. The triangular
shape of the leaves is very distinctive.

Size The leaves shown are 30mm (1.2in) across and the tree
can grow to 30 metres (97.5ft) in height.

Distribution *Ginkgo*
is found fossilized in
strata ranging in age
from Permian to
Recent. The
specimen shown is
from the Jurassic of
North Yorkshire,
UK.

Williamsonia

This is a leaf belonging to one of the most primitive of the
Cycadophytes, which are a group of Gymnosperms.
Williamsonia is noted for its pinnate leaves, clearly seen in this
example. It is an interesting plant because its flowers were
hermaphroditic (with male and female parts). It grew in
swampy or marshy conditions, and fossils are often numerous
in strata from these environments. This example is typically
preserved as a thin carbonaceous film.

Size The specimen illustrated is about 30mm (1.2in) long.

Distribution *Williamsonia* is found in rocks of Jurassic age
worldwide.

Coniopteris

This is the carbonaceous fossil of an elegant fern, characterized by a central axis with leaflets growing at an angle. The leaflets are slightly indented on the upper margins.

Size The specimen shows leaves which are 20mm (0.8in) long.

Distribution *Coniopteris* is found in rocks of Mesozoic age in northernmost North America, the CIS, India, Japan and Europe.

Acer

This delicate leaf is of the modern genus, which includes maples and sycamores. Such fossils are preserved only where there has been rapid deposition of soft, fine-grained sediment.

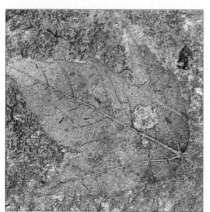

Size The specimen illustrated is 60mm (2.4in) wide.
Distribution Such trees are found worldwide and are fossilized in Late Tertiary strata. This example is from the Miocene of northern France.

Algae

These simple plants were among the first organisms to live on the earth's surface. They are classified into various subdivisions, including blue-green algae (which produced oxygen in the earth's primitive atmosphere). Many of these organisms live in the sea, and some are commonly known as seaweeds.

Stromatolite

This is a fossilized lime-rich mound secreted by blue-green algae living in shallow marine conditions. Stromatolites date back to the Pre-Cambrian age and are some of the most ancient fossils, being as old as 3,500 million years. Modern stromatolites are able to live in highly saline waters, which are unsuitable for many creatures. They produce oxygen, and before their development primitive Earth's atmosphere was anoxic.

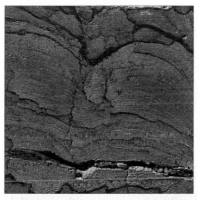

Size These fossils can be up to 500mm (20in) in height. The specimens illustrated are smaller. The single one is 20mm (0.8in) across its base, and the double mound is 100mm (4in) across. **Distribution** Stromatolites are found in rocks of Pre-Cambrian to Recent age worldwide.

Solenopora jurassica

This algal structure has clearly visible banding and in the fossil shows beautiful colours. The rock in which it is found is locally called 'beetroot stone' because of its colour. This specimen has

been cut to show the detail of the internal structure. The pink and white colour banding follows this structure, and the colouring may well be an original feature, though the banding has possibly been emphasized by leaching.

Size Specimens of this type are about 120mm (4.8in) in height.

Distribution The genus *Solenopora* has a worldwide distribution and has been found in rocks ranging from Lower Palaeozoic to Recent in age. This remarkable specimen is from the Middle Jurassic of Gloucestershire, UK.

Solenopora

A very different form of this algal genus, this species has a slender, tube-like structure. The tubes are covered with pores and have Y-shaped branches. They are composed of calcite.

Size The field of view is 40mm (1.6in) across.

Distribution The specimen illustrated is from Ordovician rocks in southern Norway, and this species of *Solenopora* ranges from Ordovician to Jurassic.

Animals - Invertebrates

Fossils belonging to this Kingdom first become numerous in the fossil record in rocks of Cambrian age. Their Pre-Cambrian ancestors may not have been able to secrete hard shells or skeletons and thus were not easily preserved.

Bryozoa *Fenestella*

This fossil bryozoan is a colonial organism related to modern sea-mats. These often live adhering to rocks or seaweed. They are common fossils, especially in limestones, where their net-like structure helps to bind the limy mud together, particularly in reef limestones developed in shallow water.

Size The specimen shown is typical at about 40mm (1.6in) across.
Distribution *Fenestella* is found in rocks ranging in age from Ordovician to Recent worldwide. The specimen is from Permian limestones in northern England.

Protozoa *Nummulites*

This is a fossil foraminiferan in the phylum Protozoa. These are microfossils that secrete a calcareous shell. Many, such as *Nummulites*, are benthonic, but a number are planktonic creatures. This example has a flattened test which is discoid and coiled in a flat spiral. Each coil is further divided by septa. Like the specimen illustrated, great numbers of the shells accumulate as limestone.

Size The individual shells average about 5mm (0.2in) in diameter.
Distribution *Nummulites* is recorded from rocks ranging in age from Palaeocene to Oligocene.

Cnidaria

Anthozoa (Corals)

Within this class there are three important groups commonly found as fossils. These are the subclasses Tabulata, Rugosa, and Zoantharia. The last of these includes the order Scleractinia, hexacorals, which are important from the Triassic onwards. The Rugosa and Tabulata are extinct.

Corals consist of a tube-shaped corallite, which has a shallow depression called a calice at the top. Here the coral-secreting polyp lived. The tube can be simple or complex, with internal horizontal divisions known as tabulae, and vertical radiating structures called septa. The corallite wall may be thickened and made stronger by web-like masses of calcite (dissepiments). Of the two extinct groups, the Tabulata are the more simple, with little internal structure apart from tabulae. The Rugosa, however, have tabulae, septa and dissepiments. Tabulate corals are always colonial, whereas the rugose corals can be solitary or colonial. The more recent scleractinian corals have similar features to the rugose group, but have their septa in groups of six rather than four. Corals are common fossils, especially in limestone rocks, which are often largely built of coral.

Halysites

This is a common genus of tabulate corals with a typical chain structure, the colonial corallites being linked in sinuous chains. These corallites have an oval or rounded section with very short septa. Tabulae divide the corallites longitudinally.
Size The field of view is 70mm (2.8in) across.
Distribution This coral is found in rocks of Middle Ordovician to Upper Silurian age worldwide.

Favosites

This is a tabulate genus with a rounded outline, and consists of many small individual corallites. These are prismatic with porous walls. They have tabulae as their internal divisions. The photograph is taken from above and shows the mass of closely joined corallites.

Size The specimen illustrated is 90mm (3.6in) in diameter.
Distribution *Favosites* is found in rocks of Upper Ordovician to Middle Devonian age worldwide. The specimen is from Silurian rocks in Shropshire, UK.

Thamnopora

This polished specimen shows the internal tabulae of the branched tabulate coral as thin, pale, calcite divisions within the individual corallites. The walls of the corallites are thick and porous.
Size The field of view is 80mm (3.2in) across.
Distribution *Thamnopora* is a genus from Devonian rocks worldwide. The specimen is from Torquay, Devon, UK.

Dibunophyllum

This specimen has been cut to show the beautiful internal structure of the corallite. It is a solitary rugose coral, and the radiating septa and web-like dissepiments can be clearly seen. There are main septa, which almost meet the axis, and discontinuous minor septa.

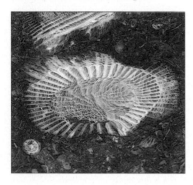

Size This coral is about 20mm (0.8in) in diameter. **Distribution** This is a genus from the Lower Carboniferous strata of North America, Asia, Europe and north Africa.

Siphonodendron

Another polished specimen that shows the internal detail. This genus is a rugose coral with well-developed septa, seen as the thin lines radiating from the centre to the edge of each corallite. The margins of the corallite are strengthened with dissepiments. It is colonial.

Size Each corallite is about 7mm (0.28in) in diameter.
Distribution *Siphonodendron* is from the Carboniferous strata of Europe.

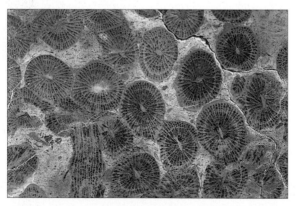

Lonsdaleia

Two specimens are shown, one of which has been sectioned to exhibit the detail of the internal structure. This is a genus of rugose corals, which grow colonially. There is a deep calice at the top of each corallite and a definite central axis runs vertically through the structure. The septa, which are well seen in both specimens, are long, and there are strengthening dissepiments around the corallite walls.

Size The individual corallites are about 8mm (0.32in) in diameter in the uncut specimen.

Distribution
This genus is found in rocks of Carboniferous age in North America, Europe, Asia, north Africa and Australia.

Syringopora

This is a colonial genus of tabulate corals, which has many long, tube-shaped corallites closely joined together by small tubular structures. The very small, pointed septa are visible in the illustration. Numerous tabulae divide the corallites vertically.

Size The specimen illustrated is 80mm (3.2in) across.

Distribution *Syringopora* is found in rocks of Upper Ordovician to Carboniferous age worldwide.

Cyathophyllum

This is a genus of solitary rugose corals that, as demonstrated in the two specimens shown, can vary in structure from

slender to cone-shaped. There are long septa and dissepiments to strengthen the corallite wall. The septa are of two types, the main ones reaching to the centre of the corallite. They can be seen in the slender specimen as thin longitudinal lines.

Size The larger specimen illustrated is 70mm (2.8in) long.

Distribution This coral occurs in rocks of Devonian age in North America, Europe, Asia and Australia.

Ketophyllum

These are two halves of the same specimen, one showing the internal structure. It is a solitary rugose coral, which has a deep calice. The corallite is cone-shaped. There are ridges on

the outside of the corallite, a typical feature of many rugose corals. This genus anchored itself to the sea bed with root-like structures, which are sometimes preserved.
Size The specimen illustrated is 80mm (3.2in) long.
Distribution *Ketophyllum* occurs in Silurian rocks in China and Europe.

Lithostrotion

This is a common rugose genus which has colonial corallites. There are tabulae and septa, and the structure has cone-shaped central parts, all of which can be seen where this specimen is broken. The mass of corallites often has a root-like appearance.
Size The specimen shown is 70mm (2.8in) across.
Distribution This coral is found in rocks of Carboniferous age in North America, Europe, north Africa and Australia.

Thysanophyllum

This is a genus of rugose corals which is colonial, with the corallites in close contact and having an angular outline. Some corallites are eight-sided, while others are six-sided. As can be seen in this specimen, the septa reach almost to the middle of the corallite and the walls are thickened with dissepiments.

Size The specimen illustrated is about 100mm (4in) across.

Distribution *Thysanophyllum* is found in rocks of Carboniferous age in Europe.

Thecosmilia

This is a Mesozoic genus of scleractinian corals with similar features to some of the rugose corals, but the septa are in groups of six. (Hexacorals is an alternative name.) This genus has corallites which may branch. There are straight septa, which can be easily seen in both illustrations. They are vertical calcite sheets that radiate from the centre of the corallite. The corallite wall is strengthened by calcite dissepiments, which can be seen most clearly in the sectioned specimen. This coral is a reef-builder, and in the same specimen there is a matrix of oolitic limestone, the small, rounded ooliths showing a typical concentric banded structure.

Size The single non-sectioned specimen shown is a maximum of 30mm (1.2in) wide.

Distribution
This genus has been discovered worldwide in rocks ranging in age from Triassic to Cretaceous.

Isastraea

This is a scleractinian coral with a colonial structure. Many of the six-sided, closely joined corallites are seen in the photograph. The whole coral is large and roughly cylindrical. The septa are in six groups, of which the longest septa are easily visible in some of the corallites in this specimen. Dissepiments strengthen the corallite walls.

Size The whole coral, of which this is a detail, is 65mm (2.6in) in height.

Distribution
The genus is from Jurassic and Cretaceous rocks in North America, Europe and Africa. The specimen illustrated is from southern England.

Thamnastrea

This sectioned specimen shows some of the typical features of this scleractinian genus. The corallite walls are not well formed, and the structure of one corallite joins with that of the next. This is especially true of the septa. A reef-building coral, the specimen is preserved in oolitic limestone. The cavity to the bottom right of the photograph contains a small scalenohedral calcite crystal.

Size The field of view is 50mm (2in).

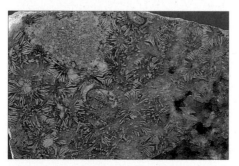

Distribution
Thamnastrea is found in rocks of Triassic to Cretaceous age in North America, South America, Europe and Asia.

Porifera

This group of organisms is somewhat difficult to classify. They are usually considered to be the forerunners of the Metazoans and are between this group and the Protozoans. Sponges are found fossilized in rocks as old as the Cambrian period, and live today in marine and non-marine waters at all depths. The sponge consists of a bag-like structure, with an opening on the upper surface and often a long stalk beneath. The skeleton is made of spicules, which are often siliceous and therefore readily preserved as fossils. These spicules provide a source of silica from which chert may well be formed. This is a hard, grey-coloured nodular material, which forms discrete masses and bands in many limestones. Some sponges have a calcareous internal framework to support their soft structures.

Raphidonema

This genus has an almost flower-like structure, with a narrow base and a wide, folded upper surface. The thick walls of this sponge contain many small pores and canals. It lives in shallow parts of the sea bed, with the narrow end in the sediment.
Size This sponge grows to about 50mm (2in) high.
Distribution It is found in rocks of Triassic to Cretaceous age in Europe. The specimen illustrated is from Cretaceous rocks of southern England.

Thamnospongia

This is a root-like structure with many irregular branches, which have a rough outer surface and are porous. The example illustrated is preserved in a flint nodule. It is thought that the silica from which flint is made may come from accumulations derived from the skeletal spicules of sponges. Flint is a type of chert, noted for its hardness and sharp curved fracture. It is common in the chalk of Britain and Europe.

Size This nodular specimen is 80mm (3.2in) in diameter.
Distribution *Thamnospongia* is found in rocks of Cretaceous age worldwide.

Ventriculites

This genus has a narrow, vase-like structure, with an anchoring 'root' system in complete specimens. There are numerous vertical and horizontal grooves on the outer surface.

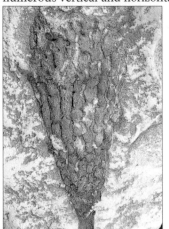

The structure is porous with internal radiating canals. This genus belongs to a group called the Hyalosporangia, which have thin walls and branching skeletons. Their modern representatives live in warm seas.
Size The specimen illustrated is 30mm (1.2in) long.
Distribution *Ventriculites* is found in Cretaceous rocks in Europe.

Laosciadia

This genus has a root-like structure and is therefore called a rhizomorine sponge. It is highly porous and rounded, and is not unlike a mushroom in appearance. This genus has, in the past, had the name *Seliscothon*, and specimens in collection may be thus labelled. It has siliceous spicules.

Size The specimen illustrated is 40mm (1.6in) in diameter.
Distribution This sponge is found in Cretaceous to Recent strata in Europe.

Siphonia

This genus has a characteristic tulip shape and is held to the sea bed by narrow 'roots', which are not often preserved as fossils. The rounded upper part of the sponge has many small pores, which are related to the internal system of canals. These

follow the overall shape of the sponge and join a large canal which extends from the upper surface to the centre of the structure. The larger canals are used for removing water from the sponge, while the smaller, radial canals bring water in.
Size The specimen illustrated is 30mm (1.2in) long.
Distribution *Siphonia* is found in rocks of Cretaceous and Tertiary age in Europe.

Echinodermata

This phylum contains the familiar Echinoids (sea urchins), which together with Asteroids (starfish), Ophiuroids (brittle stars) and Crinoids (sea lilies) are common in the fossil record. There are also four other less common classes in the phylum. These animals are characterized by an external calcareous skeleton, with a pentameral (five-fold) symmetry. They are entirely marine organisms and their history stretches back to Cambrian times.

Crinoidea (Sea-lilies)

This group of echinoderms has an almost plant-like structure, with roots, a stem and a flower-like calyx. The creature's delicate body is contained in the calyx, which is held above the sea bed by a stem made of small calcite plates called ossicles. These may be rounded, star-shaped or hexagonal, and vary considerably from species to species. The stems break easily and make up much crinoidal limestone. The base of the stem may be held to the sea-bed, or to algae, with root-like structures branching from the stem, though some crinoids are free-swimming. The calyx is made of larger calcareous plates and can be found as a whole fossil. Growing from this calyx are the arms, which may have delicate pinnules on them. These help to gather microscopic organisms on which the creature feeds.

The stems of crinoids are made up of small calcite plates called ossicles. Here many ossicles and small stem fragments have been weathered out of the limestone in which they are fossilized. The detailed structure and markings of some of these ossicles is clearly seen. They are of Carboniferous age.

Scyphocrinites

This specimen shows the calyx and branched arms of a
crinoid, which is held to the sea-bed by a bulbous 'hold-fast'.
As can be seen from the photograph, the calyx is large. The
segmented nature of the arms and branches with a structure of
joined ossicles is clearly seen. Another explanation of the

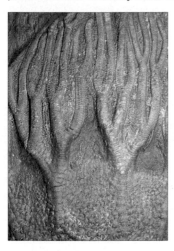

bulbous structure on the base
of the stem is that it acted as
a float, allowing the creature
to be carried by ocean
currents. Its wide
geographical distribution
confirms this possibility.
Size The specimen shown is
100mm (4in) long.
Distribution This crinoid is
found in rocks of Upper
Silurian to Devonian age in
North America, north Africa
and Europe. The specimen
illustrated is from rocks of
Devonian age in north Africa.

Clematocrinus

This specimen is of the calyx and arms of a small crinoid
genus. The arms have numerous slender branches. The fossil
shows the arms and pinnules curved towards each other, and
only a few fragments of the slender stem.
Size The example shown is 25mm (1in) long.
Distribution *Clematocrinus* is found in rocks of Middle
Silurian age in North America, Europe and Australia.

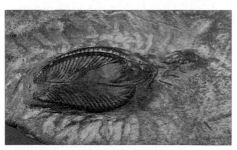

Macrocrinus

This crinoid genus has 12-16 stout arms rising above the small calyx. Here they are fossilized with the pinnules. These almost feathery structures form an open funnel around the mouth. Each pinnule and the minute cirri upon it make up a food-gathering net; the mouth is deep at the centre of the calyx.

Size A small crinoid, the larger specimen illustrated being 40mm (1.6in) long.

Distribution This genus is found in Lower Carboniferous rocks in North America.

Woodocrinus

The calyx and arms of this crinoid are shown here. The arms are quite thick and branch into two or four just above the level

of the calyx. The ossicles are circular, and the genus has a short, tapering stem. The stem lacks roots, so the creature may have drifted in the water.

Size The specimen illustrated is 40mm (1.6in) across.

Distribution *Woodocrinus* is found in rocks of Carboniferous age in Europe. The specimen is from North Yorkshire, UK.

Encrinus

This crinoid has a small calyx, and the plated structure is clearly seen in the photograph. The stem has a circular cross-section, but none of this is visible here. The arms are strong and pinnulate. The typical echinoderm 'zigzag' suturing between the plates can be seen on the arms.

Size This specimen is typical at 35mm (1.4in) in length.
Distribution *Encrinus* is found in Middle and Upper Triassic rocks in Europe (but not the UK), and is well known in Germany.

Pentacrinites

A characteristic feature of this genus is the star shape of the stem ossicles. These are often found singly in shales and limestones. The calyx is small and there are long arms, seen in this example, which have pinnules and cirri. The stem can be very long. Modern species in this genus live off the sea-bed. The arms shown in the photograph are preserved in pyrite.

Size The stem can be over 1 metre (39in) long. The part shown here is 20mm (0.8in) long.
Distribution *Pentacrinites* occurs in rocks of Triassic to Pliocene age in North America and Europe.

Echinoidea (Sea-urchins)

This class contains the sea-urchins, well known for their spiny shells and rounded shape. However, the whole shell, or test, can vary considerably, from rounded to heart-shaped, flattened to dome-shaped. The spines may be thin, numerous and sharp, few and bulbous, or club-shaped. The test, in which the soft body of the animal is housed, is made of two types of calcareous plates. These are the larger interambulacral plates and the smaller ambulacral plates, which make alternating bands running round the test from the oral surface (below) to the aboral surface (above). The test has a pentameral symmetry in many genera, especially in those referred to as the regular echinoids. The irregular echinoids tend to have bilateral symmetry, and the ambulacral areas, for example, may be atrophied and not reach right round the test. The ambulacral plates are covered in pores, which have small tube-feet passing through them. These delicate, flower-like structures are used for movement, feeding and respiration. In the regular echinoids the mouth is below and the anus is on the upper surface. The irregular forms may have these important features on the side on the test. Echinoids are adapted to many marine environments, and first appear in rocks of Ordovician age. They are common sea creatures today.

Plegiocidaris

This regular echinoid has large bosses on its test to which the stout spines are attached with a ball and socket joint. The mouth is centrally placed on the under surface and the anus is central above. This view from the side of the test shows the ambulacral areas between the boss-bearing interambulacral plates.

Size The genus is about 30mm (1.2in) in diameter.
Distribution *Plegiocidaris* is found in rocks of Upper Triassic to Upper Jurassic age in Europe.

Cidaris

The specimen illustrated has been preserved with many of its long, thick spines. The test has been broken, but the bosses where the spines were attached are still visible in places. Usually, preservation is of the test only, and the spines are found as isolated fossils. This is a regular echinoid with a rounded test, and the mouth and anus centrally placed.
Size The specimen shown is about 30mm (1.2in) in diameter.
Distribution *Cidaris* is found in rocks of Jurassic to Recent age worldwide.

Clypeus

A relatively large echinoid, *Clypeus* is irregular and the anus is not central, but placed posteriorly in a groove on the upper surface of the test. This gives the test a bilateral symmetry. It

has a flattened shape and the ambulacra are entire and slightly petaloid. The interambulacra are porous.
Size The specimen shown is typical at 70mm (2.8in) in diameter.
Distribution This genus is found in rocks of Jurassic age in Europe, Africa and Australia.

Pygaster

This irregular echinoid has bilateral symmetry, and the anus is in an oval area on the upper surface, clearly seen in the photograph. The interambulacra are broad and the ambulacral bands thin. There are small tubercles covering the test, which has a pentagonal outline.

Size The specimen illustrated is 60mm (2.4in) in diameter.
Distribution *Pygaster* is found in rocks of Jurassic and Cretaceous age in Europe.

Holectypus

This echinoid has a circular test, but is an irregular genus because the anus is not centrally placed. The underneath (oral surface) is flat or slightly concave, and there are large tubercles on this surface. The ambulacra are reasonably straight. When seen from the side, the test is slightly domed.
Size The specimen shown is typical at 20mm (0.8in) in diameter.

Distribution This genus is found in strata of Lower Jurassic to Upper Cretaceous age in North America, Europe, north Africa, Venezuela and Japan.

Micraster

This is a common genus of irregular, heart-shaped echinoids. Both the oral (left) and aboral surfaces are shown. The ambulacra are petaloid and atrophied. The anus is placed posteriorly, high on the test, with a slight ridge above it. The mouth is below, on the oral surface, and there is a notch or groove in the anterior part of the shell near the mouth.

Size The genus is usually about 50mm (2in) in diameter.
Distribution It is found in rocks of Cretaceous to Palaeocene age worldwide.

Holaster

This genus is irregular and has a rounded test with a slight point at the posterior end. The anus is on the posterior side of the test. The ambulacra are petaloid, and the interambulacral areas broad. The pores are paired and almost like small slits in the test. There are small tubercles on the upper surface and larger ones below. This genus is thought to be related to *Echinocorys*, but differs in that *Holaster* has a distinctively heart-shaped test.

Size The specimen illustrated is typical at 90mm (3.6in) in diameter.
Distribution *Holaster* is found in rocks of Lower Cretaceous to Eocene age worldwide. The specimen is from Kent, UK.

Hemipneustes

This genus grows to a large size and is irregular. The test is rounded or ovoid and has a domed side-view. The periproct, a group of plates containing the anus, is on the posterior side of the test, and the mouth is anterior, giving the irregular echinoid's typical bilateral symmetry. An interesting feature is the groove on the test in which one of the ambulacra is situated.

Size The specimen illustrated is about 60mm (2.4in) in diameter.
Distribution *Hemipneustes* is found in rocks of Cretaceous age in northern Europe.

Echinocorys

This echinoid is irregular and has a wide, flat base and domed upper surface. The anus is below, but at the posterior end. A ridge runs across the test between the mouth and anus. The ambulacra are quite straight and porous, while the wide interambulacra have small tubercles.

Size The specimen is 80mm (3.2in) in diameter.
Distribution *Echinocorys* is found in Upper Cretaceous rocks in North America, Europe, Asia Minor, Madagascar and Cuba.

Cassidulus

This small genus is irregular, and the ambulacra are only just visible on the specimen illustrated. These are atrophied and petaloid, forming a star shape on the aboral surface. The outline of the test is sub-rounded, but has a roughly pentameral shape. The anus is posteriorly sited.

Size *Cassidulus* is about 40mm (1.6in) in diameter.
Distribution It is found in rocks of Eocene to Recent age worldwide.

Dendraster

With an oval test outline, this is an irregular genus. The petaloid, atrophied ambulacra stop short of the test margin, and have slit-like pores. The periproct, containing the anus, is marginal, and there is a groove above the anus.

Size This genus reaches about 40mm (1.6in) in diameter.
Distribution It is found in Pliocene and Recent strata in North America.

Lovenia

This irregular genus is characterized by a heart-shaped test with a definite groove at the anterior end. The ambulacra are short (atrophied), and have wide notches along their margins. The test has a rough surface, and the tubercles, to which spines are attached, are recessed.

Size The specimen illustrated is about 30mm (1.2in) in diameter.
Distribution This genus occurs in rocks of Eocene to Recent age in Australia.

Amphiope

This rather strange, flattened, irregular echinoid has a rounded test with two distinct notches in the posterior end. The oral surface *(right)* is covered with small pores and has Y-shaped grooves radiating from the mouth. The aboral surface *(left)* has short petaloid ambulacra that form a 'feathery' star shape. The anus is on the posterior margin of the oral surface.
Size This genus reached about 30mm (1.2in) in diameter.
Distribution *Amphiope* is found in rocks of Oligocene to Miocene age in Europe and India.

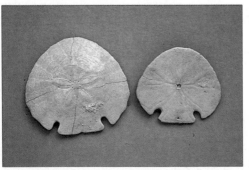

Parmulechinus

This small, disc-like, irregular echinoid has a very flattened
test. The atrophied, petaloid ambulacra form a star-shaped
pattern on the aboral surface. The mouth is centrally placed
on the underside of the test. There are pores along the margins
of the ambulacra, and the interambulacral areas are broad and
made of large plates.

Size The specimens
illustrated are typical at
15mm (0.6in) in diameter.
Distribution
Parmulechinus is found in
rocks of Oligocene age in
Europe and north Africa.

Encope

The test of this irregular echinoid is sub-circular, with a slight
pentameral outline, and is characterized by holes at the end of
the petaloid ambulacra. There is another hole in the aboral
surface in a posterior direction from the centre. The
ambulacra are atrophied and have slit-like pores along their
margins. The underside of the test (the oral surface) contains
the mouth and anus, and has five pairs of wavy grooves, the
ends of which contain the holes related to the ambulacra.

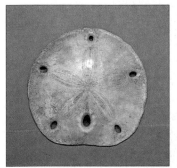

Size The specimen
illustrated is 90mm (3.6in)
in diameter.
Distribution This genus is
found in Miocene to Recent
strata in North America,
South America and the West
Indies. The specimen
illustrated is from Pleistocene
rocks in San Diego,
California, USA.

Clypeaster

This large irregular genus has a rounded test, with five distinct lobes on its margins related to the ambulacra, which are bulbous and petaloid and have slit-like pores on their margins. The mouth and anus are on the oral surface, the anus at the posterior margin.

Size The specimen illustrated is 70mm (2.8in) in diameter.
Distribution *Clypeaster* occurs in rocks of Upper Eocene to Recent age worldwide.

Asteroidea (Starfish)

These are the starfish, and they have a very similar five-fold symmetry to many other echinoderms. It is not common to find them preserved entire because of their delicate structure. They are first found in the fossil record in Ordovician strata, and many species live in modern oceans.

Lapworthura

This is an Ophiuroid, or brittle star, and has a central disc with five flexible arms radiating from it. The structure is made of ossicles.
Size It reached about 50mm (2in) in diameter.

Distribution This starfish is found in rocks of Ordovician and Silurian age in Europe and Australia. The specimen illustrated is from northern England.

Palaeocoma

This is another genus of brittle stars. It is a common fossil, and the structure of a central disc and slender arms made of diamond-shaped plates is well shown in this fine specimen. *Palaeocoma* is closely related to the modern brittle stars (Ophiuroids).

Size The central disc is up to 20mm (0.8in) in diameter.

Distribution *Palaeocoma* is a genus from the Jurassic and Cretaceous rocks of Europe, and in favourable conditions was fossilized in great numbers.

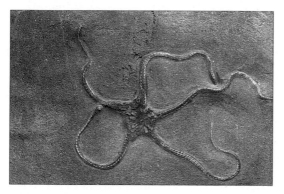

Metopaster

This strange fossil echinoderm is an asteroid, but lacks the arms typical of these organisms. It has a pentagonal perimeter of large plates, and numerous smaller ones within. These form the oral and aboral surfaces.

Size The genus has a maximum diameter of about 60mm (2.4in).

Distribution It is found in Cretaceous to Miocene rocks in Europe.

Brachiopoda

This phylum of shelled marine creatures has had far more representatives at certain times in the past than it has today. Brachiopods first appear in the fossil record during the Cambrian period, and, like many other groups of organisms, they must have developed from soft-bodied Pre-Cambrian ancestors. At first glance a brachiopod shell resembles that of a bivalve mollusc, but apart from the fact that both groups of fossils have two shells, there is little similarity. The brachiopod shell is made of two valves which are dissimilar. One, the pedicle valve, is usually larger and has an opening in the posterior end through which protruded, in life, a fleshy stalk called the pedicle. This anchored the animal to the sea-bed. The pointed end of the shell where the pedicle opening is situated is the umbo or 'beak'. The smaller valve is called the brachial valve and contains a curved, ciliated organ, the lophophore, on which food (in the sea water drawn into the shell) was trapped. In some fossils the brachidium, a calcareous support for the soft lophophore, is preserved.

Two classes of brachiopods are recognized. The more primitive Inarticulata were unable to move their two valves relative to each other. Many of the early Cambrian species are in this group. The Articulata have a mechanism of hinge and muscles for opening and closing the shell. This phylum became adapted to living in many sea-bed environments; some burrowed, others were fixed to rocks.

Lingulella

This brachiopod has an almost oval shell outline, with no external ornamentation. The inside of the valves, the surface of which is seen in the fossils illustrated, has numerous fine lines. *Lingulella* was a burrower and had a long pedicle that held it fast to the floor of its burrow. This slab of slate shows many disarticulated valves, which have separated before fossilization. The genus belongs to the class Inarticulata.

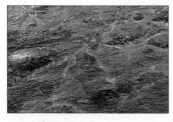

Size *Lingulella* grew to about 30mm (1.2in) in length.
Distribution This creature is found in shallow-water marine rocks of Cambrian to Ordovician age worldwide. The specimen shown is from Porthmadog, Wales.

Lingula

Another genus of inarticulate brachiopods, *Lingula* has an oval shell outline, and the valves are ornamented with numerous fine ribs and growth lines. In the fossils illustrated some of the shell material still remains as a whitish covering. This brachiopod burrowed into the sea-bed and had a pedicle as long as the shell.

Size The genus grows to about 30mm (1.2in) in length.
Distribution It is found in rocks ranging in age from Ordovician to Recent and is one of the longest surviving genera. It occurs worldwide. The specimen illustrated is of Carboniferous age from Northumberland, UK.

Orthis

This articulate brachiopod has an almost rounded shell outline with a short hinge line. The pedicle valve has a convex shape, and the brachial one is flat or slightly convex. On this slab of micaceous sandstone some internal shell structures are preserved, along with the ribbed external surfaces of the valves.

Size It grew to about 20mm (0.8in) in width.
Distribution *Orthis* is a common brachiopod from rocks of Ordovician age worldwide.

Heterorthis

This genus of brachiopod has a pedicle valve which is convex, but the brachial valve is flat. The overall outline of the shell is sub-circular, and the outer surface of the valves is ornamented with fine ribs. The specimen illustrated shows the common preservation of the internal part of the shell. *Heterorthis* is an articulate brachiopod.

Size A shell which grew to about 35mm (1.4in) in diameter.
Distribution It is found in rocks of Ordovician age worldwide.

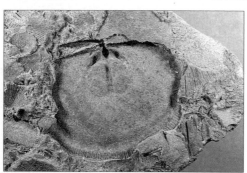

Sowerbyella

This articulate brachiopod has a straight hinge line and a shell of semi-circular outline. The outside of the shell is ornamented with radiating ribs. Both specimens shown are internal moulds with some external shell surfaces. The pedicle valve is convex, and the brachial valve concave.

Size A small genus, growing to only 15mm (0.6in) in diameter.
Distribution It is found in rocks of Ordovician age worldwide.

Leptaena

This brachiopod belongs to the class Articulata, and has much shell ornamentation consisting of ribs and wavy concentric ridges. The pedicle valve is convex, and the brachial valve is flat. The outline is semicircular and there are 'ears' on the straight hinge line. *Leptaena* lay on the sea floor with the pedicle valve beneath. Three specimens are illustrated on a block of Silurian limestone.

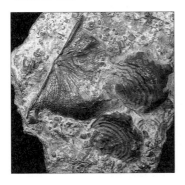

Size The genus grew to about 50mm (2.0in) wide.
Distribution It is found in rocks of Ordovician to Devonian age worldwide.

Spirifer

This brachiopod shell has a semicircular outline with a prominent, straight hinge line. In the specimen illustrated the beak of the pedicle valve can be seen protruding above the hinge line. The surface of the valves is heavily ornamented with ribs and growth lines. A groove can be seen in the brachial valve, running from the beak to the shell margin.

Size *Spirifer* grew quite large, reaching up to 120mm (4.8in) in width.
Distribution This articulate brachiopod is found in strata of Carboniferous age worldwide.

Orbiculoidea

This genus belongs to the class Inarticulata. It has a rounded outline. Both valves are shown in the photograph. Each is conical in shape and was made of chitin and phosphates rather than calcareous material. The ornamentation consists of growth lines and there is a slit for the pedicle.

Size The shell has a width of about 20mm (0.8in).

Distribution It is found in strata of Ordovician to Permian age worldwide.

Schizophoria

This articulate brachiopod shell has an almost rectangular outline. Both valves are convex, although the brachial valve is more curved. Each is shown in the illustration, the darker valve on the left being the pedicle valve. There is little surface ornamentation, apart from fine ribs.

Size *Schizophoria* grew to about 50mm (2.0in) in width.

Distribution A genus from rocks of Silurian to Permian age worldwide. The specimen is from Carboniferous strata in northern France.

Productus

This is a well-known articulate genus, which has a very convex pedicle valve and a concave or flat brachial valve. The shell surface is ornamented with numerous ribs, and there are wavy growth lines. The hinge line is short and straight. The pedicle valve is shown in the photograph.

Size A genus that grew to about 40mm (1.6in) in width.
Distribution It is found in rocks of Carboniferous age in Europe and Asia. The specimen illustrated is from Carboniferous limestone in Derbyshire, UK.

Pustula

An articulate brachiopod with an almost rectangular outline, this genus is not unlike *Productus* in appearance. There are numerous growth lines reflecting the shell outline, as well as faint ribs radiating from the beak. The pedicle valve is convex and the brachial valve is flat.
Size This genus grew to about 120mm (4.8in) in width.
Distribution It is found in Carboniferous strata in Europe. The specimen illustrated is from Staffordshire, UK.

Unispirifer

This articulate brachiopod has a bi-convex shell and is ornamented with radiating ribs. Some of these bifurcate (split in two). The hinge line is straight and is the widest part of the shell. In the photograph the beak of the larger pedicle valve is seen behind the brachial valve.

Size *Unispirifer* grew to about 120mm (4.8in) in width.
Distribution It is found in Carboniferous strata worldwide.

Stenoscisma

This small articulate brachiopod is characterized by its pointed beak and strongly ribbed valves. The overall shell shape is ovoid. The examples shown are internal casts, the shell having been dissolved away.
Size A genus which reached only 20mm (0.8in) in diameter.
Distribution It occurs in rocks of Devonian to Permian age in Europe. These specimens are from the Permian reef limestones of Durham, UK.

Stiphrothyris

This articulate genus has an elongated, ovoid shell with an obvious pedicle opening. There are faint growth lines as ornamentation, and a fold or sulcus occurs in the anterior part of the shell. In the specimen illustrated the brachial valve has been opened to reveal the calcareous loop which supported the lophophore during life. This organ had a two-fold purpose. It produced water currents which entered the shell, and also caught food particles which were transferred to the mouth.

Size *Stiphrothyris* grew to about 40mm (1.6in) in length.
Distribution It is found in Middle Jurassic strata in Europe. In these rocks this genus was attached to the sea-bed by its fleshy pedicle. It is often fossilized in limestones, which were found in shallow conditions. These rocks are commonly oolitic.

Tetrarhynchia

This is a typical genus of Mesozoic articulate brachiopods, with a small, sub-triangular shell. It is ornamented with many strong ribs, and there is a pronounced zigzag fold in the margin of the shell. The umbo is small and pointed.

Size The genus has a maximum shell width of about 20mm (0.8in).
Distribution This brachiopod is found in rocks of Jurassic age in North America and Europe.

Goniorhynchia

A brachiopod belonging to the class Articulata, *Goniorhynchia* has a sub-triangular shell outline and the valves are both convex. The pedicle valve is slightly larger than the brachial valve. The small, sharp beak has the pedicle opening below it. The shell surface is ornamented with strong ribs that radiate from the beak. There is a fold in the anterior part of the pedicle valve.

Size This brachiopod grew to about 30mm (1.2in) in width.
Distribution The genus occurs in rocks of Jurassic age in Europe.

Isjuminella

A rather strangely shaped, articulate brachiopod genus with strongly curved valves, giving the shell a globose appearance. The valves are thick and ornamented with strong ribs. There are also zigzag-shaped lines around the shell, which follow the pattern of the valve margins.

Size This genus grew to about 100mm (4in) wide.
Distribution It is found in rocks of Jurassic age in the CIS and Europe.

Terebratella

This brachiopod genus, a member of the class Articulata, has an oval shell outline and a pedicle valve slightly larger than the brachial valve. Both valves are convex. The pedicle opening can be seen just below the beak. It is well ornamented with ribs, some of which bifurcate. There are also concentric growth lines.

Size *Terebratella* grew to about 40mm (1.6in) in length.
Distribution A genus found worldwide in rocks ranging from Jurassic to Recent. The specimen illustrated is of Cretaceous age and was collected in France.

Cyclothyris

This articulate brachiopod has a sub-triangular shell outline with a small beak and pedicle opening, seen in the specimen on the right. Each valve is convex, and the brachial valve has a definite fold. There are numerous strong ribs and some fine growth lines.
Size A genus which grew to 30mm (1.2in) wide.
Distribution It is found in rocks of Cretaceous age in North America and Europe. The specimen shown is from Devon, UK.

Torquirhynchia

This articulate brachiopod shell has a sub-rounded outline, only the pointed beak area interrupting this circular appearance. Both valves are convex in shape and the pedicle opening is simple. The shell is ornamented with stout ribs which radiate from the beak. The pedicle valve (seen behind) is slightly larger than the brachial valve.

Size The shell grew to about 40mm (1.6in) wide.
Distribution *Torquirhynchia* is found in rocks of Upper Jurassic age in the CIS, and in Europe west of the Alps.

Plectothyris

An articulate brachiopod, which has a rounded shell margin, except for the triangular area towards the beak. The valves are both convex. Near the anterior margin of the shell (the opposite end to the beak) the valves are ornamented with stout ribs. The large pedicle opening is clearly seen in the photograph, where the pedicle valve projects behind the brachial valve.

Size *Plectothyris* grew to about 40mm (1.6in) wide.
Distribution This genus is found in Jurassic strata in the UK.

Pseudoglossothyris

This large articulate brachiopod has a virtually smooth shell, the only ornamentation being fine, concentric growth lines. Each valve is of convex shape, and the overall shell outline is ovoid. The large pedicle opening can be seen where the beak of the pedicle valve projects behind the smaller and more rounded brachial valve.

Size A genus which grew to 100mm (4in) in length. **Distribution** It is found in rocks of Middle Jurassic age in Europe. The specimen illustrated is from Gloucestershire, UK.

Kingena

A small, globose, articulate brachiopod with very convex valves, though the brachial valve is flatter. The pedicle opening is relatively large. There is little ornamentation on the smooth shell, apart from fine growth lines. The brachial valve has a shallow, broad fold.

Size A genus which reached only 30mm (1.2in) in diameter. **Distribution** It is found in strata of Cretaceous age worldwide. The specimens illustrated are from Texas, USA.

Morrisithyris

This articulate brachiopod shell is elongated and almost wedge-shaped. It is characterized by a broad, deep fold in the anterior part of the brachial valve, clearly seen in the photograph. There is a definite triangular outline to the posterior part of the shell, which has little ornamentation, apart from growth lines. This genus was attached to the sea-

bed by its pedicle, and is commonly found in shallow-water oolitic limestone formed on the Jurassic continental shelves.

Size A large genus, it reached 60mm (2.4in) in length.

Distribution *Morrisithyris* is found in rocks of Jurassic age in Europe.

Pygope

This strangely shaped, articulate brachiopod has a triangular outline. The edges of the shell are very steep, and a groove runs through the middle of the brachial valve, seen on the right. This groove develops into a hole. The shell can have a two-lobed appearance in some species.

Size A large genus which grew to 80mm (3.2in) in length.

Distribution It is found in rocks of Cretaceous age in Europe. The specimens shown are from Verona, Italy.

Hemichordata
Graptolithina (Graptolites)

These strange fossils belong to an extinct marine group of creatures. The graptolites were colonial organisms living in small cups (thecae) on a branching structure called a rhabdosome. This is made of one or more branches (stipes). The thecae vary considerably from one genus to another, and the general form of these and other parts of the rhabdosome is of diagnostic value. For instance, a broad division is made into biserial (thecae on both sides of the stipe) and uniserial (thecae on one side of the stipe) graptolites. The whole structure is rarely more than a few centimetres long. The earliest graptolites, such as *Dictyonema*, are many-branched and were probably benthonic (living on the sea-bed). Later forms which developed in the Ordovician period took on a planktonic existence and had larger and fewer thecae. Graptolites became extinct during the Carboniferous period.

Dictyonema

This is one of the earliest of the graptolites, and had a rhabdosome made up of numerous branches forming (when alive) a cone-shaped net structure. The multitude of stipes is joined by transverse dissepiments.

Size The structure can vary from 20 to 250mm (0.8 to 10in) in length.

Distribution Ranging through strata of Cambrian to Carboniferous age, this genus has a worldwide distribution.

Phyllograptus

This genus has leaf-like stipes which usually become separated in fossils, though in life they were joined together in fours. The thecae are tube-shaped.

Size The single stipe shown is about 20mm (0.8in) long.
Distribution *Phyllograptus* comes from rocks of Lower Ordovician age worldwide.

Didymograptus

This graptolite has the characteristic tuning-fork shape, with two stipes joined in a V. The stipes are uniserial, with thecae on only one side. These thecae are tube-shaped. The genus is thought to have had a planktonic existence, and in some areas it is fossilized in great numbers, especially in fine-grained sedimentary rocks such as shales and mudstones. As they are such delicate organisms, fossil graptolites are usually restricted to the finer-grained sedimentary rocks.

Size *Didymograptus* can be 20 to 600mm (0.8 to 24in) in length.

Distribution It is found in rocks of Ordovician age worldwide. *Didymograptus* is used as a zone fossil.

Climacograptus

This genus has a biserial structure, with thecae on both sides of the single stipe. The thecae are sigmoidal (S-shaped), and have upward-facing apertures. It is thought to have been a planktonic graptolite with a vertical position in the water.
Size The specimen shown is typical at 20mm (0.8in) in length.
Distribution A genus from Ordovician and Silurian strata, found worldwide. This graptolite is especially common in the

Normanskill formation of New York State, and the Birkhill shales of southern Scotland.
It is used as a zone fossil for parts of the Ordovician period.

Monograptus

With a uniserial rhabdosome, this genus has very variable thecae. In some species they are simple, while in others they are hook-shaped or sigmoidal. The single stipe is usually straight, but can be curved or coiled, as in the photograph here.
Size This graptolite is between 30 and 750mm (1.2 and 30in) in length.
Distribution It is found worldwide in rocks ranging in age from Silurian to Devonian. *Monograptus* is a zone fossil for Silurian strata.

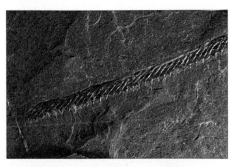

Arthropoda

This phylum includes creatures such as spiders and insects, scorpions, crabs, lobsters and ostracods. There have been many successful groups in the past that we know about only from fossils. Possibly the best known of these is the sub-phylum Trilobita (trilobites). Other fossil groups include the eurypterids, some of which grew to great size. Arthropods are characterized by an exoskeleton which is segmented. This can be articulated by the creature; trilobites, for example, can enroll like modern wood-lice (see p. 82). As an arthropod grows, the exoskeleton is moulted in a process called ecdysis. The exoskeleton is made of chitin (similar to the material of fingernails), which is strengthened by the addition of calcium phosphate and calcite.

Arthropods are first recorded as fossils in rocks of Cambrian age, and since that time they have adapted to almost every environment – in the ocean and fresh water, on the land surface and in the sky.

Sub-phylum Trilobita (Trilobites)

The trilobites were first found as fossils in strata of Cambrian age, and they are used as zone fossils for the Cambrian system. That these complex organisms occur in the Cambrian rocks with no fossilized ancestors is a matter of great interest to palaeontologists. Possibly the trilobites evolved from soft-bodied, Pre-Cambrian arthropods, which have left no trace in the fossil record. The trilobites were a most successful group as a whole, living through more than 300 million years, until they became extinct during the Permian period.

From studying their detailed structure and the strata in which they are found, it is believed that trilobites lived on or near the sea-bed. Certain genera may have been active swimmers, while others burrowed in the soft mud of the sea floor. The exoskeleton is very complicated and segmented. It can be enrolled, as in *Calymene* (see p. 82), but the purpose of this is debatable. Certainly this function can be for defence against predators, and modern arthropods use it as such. Other structures on the exoskeleton in the form of spines and tubercles may also have put off aggressors. Another use of enrolment may have been during times of little food, provided the organism was capable of slowing down its metabolic rate.

The name trilobite is derived from the structure of the exoskeleton, which is divided longitudinally into three lobes. There is a central axial lobe and two lateral lobes, one on either side. These are all segmented and constructed of ribs called pleurae. The head-shield is the cephalon, and this probably contained the centre of the nervous system. The middle section of the cephalon, following the axis, is the glabella, on either side of which are the eyes, if present. These were compound in structure, composed of many delicate calcite lenses, which are sometimes wonderfully preserved in fossils. Some species had 360-degree vision, and because of this great advantage were very active swimmers, living off the sea floor. Others had eyes on stalks and may have burrowed in the sea bed; some genera were blind.

The tail section of the exoskeleton is the pygidium. This has the same general structure as the thorax, though the pygidium tapers and may have a spinose tip. In order to grow, the trilobite had to moult, as is the case with other arthropods. This process makes it possible for one trilobite to produce a number of fossils.

Trilobite fossils are often fragmented – a result of the articulation and natural breaking of the exoskeleton, especially into cephalon, thorax and pygidium. Cephalons and pygidia are the most frequently found fossils. Some, such as *Triarthrus*, have shown preservation of appendages like antennae and segmented, feathery legs. Larval trilobites (protaspides) have also been found. These consist of a single shield-like structure about 1mm (0.04in) long. The largest trilobites grew to about 1 metre (39in) in length, while the smallest species were only 1 or 2 mm (0.04 to 0.08in) long. Fossil trilobites are found in various types of sedimentary rock, especially shales and limestones.

Paradoxides and *Peronopsis*

These two very different genera show some of the great diversity within the sub-phylum Trilobita. This diversity suggests that different trilobites adopted a variety of habitats. *Paradoxides* may be very large. The specimen illustrated is over 300mm (12in) in length and has many long, spinose segments. *Peronopsis* is diminutive, 8mm (0.32in) long, with only two thoracic segments.

Paradoxides

The thorax of this genus has over 15 segments, and the pleurae are often tapering and spinose. The genal spines, extending from the base of the cephalon, may be over half the length of the thorax. There is a gradual tapering of the thorax to a very small pygidium. On the cephalon, beside the rounded glabella, there are crescentric eyes.

Size This genus is one of the largest of the trilobites, growing to over 500mm (20in) in length. The specimen shown is 85mm (3.4in) long **Distribution** *Paradoxides* is found in strata of Cambrian age in Europe, North and South America, Turkey and north Africa. The specimen illustrated is from Germany.

Ellipsocephalus

This genus has a very broad, pronounced cephalon with a narrow border. The glabella is large and rounded. There are 12 segments in the thorax, and the pygidium is small but wide. The illustration shows two fossil exoskeletons and an impression where a third trilobite shell was pressed into the soft sea-bed.
Size The specimens illustrated are a typical size of about 35mm (1.4in) long.

Distribution
Ellipsocephalus is found in strata of Lower Cambrian age in north Africa, Europe and Australia. The specimen illustrated is from Jince, Czechoslovakia.

Eodiscus

This trilobite has only three segments in its thorax, the cephalon and pygidium being relatively large and of the same size. The glabella is narrow and has a deep furrow on either side. This genus is often fossilized in fragments, as illustrated here showing isolated pygidia and cephalons. *Eodiscus* had no eyes.

Size This genus reached up to 10mm (0.4in) long. **Distribution** *Eodiscus* is found in rocks of Cambrian age in Europe and eastern North America. The specimen shown is from South Wales.

Ogygopsis

This genus has a long, deeply furrowed glabella in the centre of the cephalon. There are many thoracic segments. The pygidium has a narrow border and is slightly larger than the cephalon. In complete specimens (the one illustrated being damaged), there are short genal spines running down from the cephalon. The axial lobe tapers very gradually towards the pygidium.

Size *Ogygopsis* grew up to 100mm (4in) long.
Distribution A genus from the Cambrian strata of North America. The specimen shown is from the Burgess shale of British Columbia, Canada.

Olenellus

This genus has a slight groove down the centre of the thorax. There are distinct genal spines, and also spines on many of the thoracic segments, which are clearly shown in the specimen illustrated. There is a large cephalon, and the eyes, on either side of the glabella, are crescent-shaped. The glabella has furrows and the pygidium is small.

Size Reaching a maximum of about 80mm (3.2in) long, *Olenellus* is a medium-sized trilobite.
Distribution This trilobite is found in rocks of Cambrian age in Scotland, Greenland and North America. The specimen shown is from Pennsylvania, USA.

Agnostus

A genus which has only two thoracic segments, *Agnostus* is frequently found fragmented, as in the specimens illustrated. The cephalon and pygidium are the same size, and the glabella has a furrow running across it. Both the cephalon and pygidium have broad borders. *Agnostus* is a blind genus.
Size A very small trilobite, reaching only about 10mm (0.4in) in length.

Distribution This genus is found in strata of Cambrian age worldwide. The specimen illustrated is from Vastergotland, Sweden.

Peronopsis

Another very small genus, with a similar general appearance to *Agnostus*. There are only two thoracic segments, and the pygidium is about the same size as the cephalon. *Peronopsis* has grooves in both the cephalon and pygidium, and the glabella is cut across by a furrow. There are distinct borders to the cephalon and pygidium.

Size A very small trilobite, reaching only about 8mm (0.32in) in length.

Distribution *Peronopsis* is found in strata of Cambrian age in Europe, Siberia and North America. The specimen shown is from Montana, USA.

Solenopleura

This genus has a thorax with 14 segments, and the cephalon contains a glabella, which tapers and has a very deep furrow on either side. There is a wide border to the cephalon. The broad pygidium has 7-8 segments.

Size A genus of small- to medium-sized trilobites, which grew to 50mm (2in) in length.

Distribution *Solenopleura* is found in strata of Middle Cambrian age in North America, New Zealand, Europe and Asia.

Elrathia

A common genus from certain North America strata, *Elrathia* has 13 thoracic segments and a pygidium smaller than the cephalon. There are short genal spines extending from the margin of the cephalon where it meets the thorax. The eyes are beside the glabella, which has slight furrows across it.
Size This genus reached about 30mm (1.2in) in length.

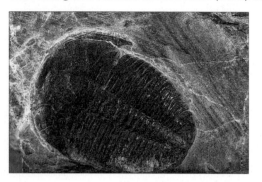

Distribution *Elrathia* is from Cambrian strata in North America. The specimen shown is from Utah, USA.

Meneviella

Only the isolated cephalon of this genus is shown. As is often the case with trilobites, the segmented exoskeleton became disjointed before fossilization took place. The cephalon is about one quarter of the whole of this animal. The surface of the cephalon is covered with radiating striations, seen in the photograph, and the glabella is narrow and tapering, with grooves separating it into segments.
Size A medium-sized genus, reaching about 60mm (2.4in) long.

Distribution This trilobite is from Middle Cambrian strata in eastern North America, Britain, Denmark and Asia.

Trinucleus

This genus has a large cephalon and the glabella has a pronounced frontal lobe. There is a fringe with radiating grooves around the cephalon. Very long genal spines developed, but these are usually broken off in fossils. The thorax has six segments, and there is a very short, wide pygidium.

Size A small trilobite, growing up to 30mm (1.2in) long.
Distribution Found in Ordovician strata in the CIS, England and Wales. The specimen shown is from Wales.

Ogyginus

This genus has a cephalon and pygidium of the same size; the pygidium is the more pointed of the two. There is a large glabella with ovoid eyes on either side. Long genal spines developed from the cephalon, which extend beside the thorax. These spines are often missing in fossils, but can be seen on the specimen illustrated. There are eight thoracic segments.

Size *Ogyginus* grew up to 40mm (1.6in) in length.
Distribution A genus from the Ordovician strata of Europe. The specimen illustrated is from Wales.

Ogygiocarella

This genus has been given a number of different names in the past. It has been called *Ogigia* and *Ogigiocaris*, and these names will still be found in some of the literature and museum collections. There is a broad, short cephalon with a large glabella, which has a central restriction. The eyes are crescent-shaped. The pygidium is larger than the cephalon and has a narrow axis which tapers markedly.

Size A genus that grew up to 80mm (3.2in) in length.
Distribution *Ogygiocarella* is found in rocks of Ordovician age in Europe and South America.

Illaenus

This genus is characterized by a very broad, smooth cephalon and pygidium, which are the same size as each other; the pygidium is without segmentation. A distinct groove marks the pygidium, following the outline of the skeleton. There are 10 thoracic segments, and this is the only part of the trilobite which is segmented.

Size *Illaenus* grew up to 50mm (2in) long.
Distribution This trilobite is found in rocks of Ordovician age worldwide. The specimen shown is from Oporto in Portugal.

Triarthrus

This genus is of great interest because specimens in North America have been found with preservation of the soft parts, including antennae and other appendages. It has 12-16 thoracic segments, and a small triangular pygidium with five segments. The semicircular cephalon has wide borders, and the glabella is segmented. There are very small eyes.

Size This trilobite grew up to 30mm (1.2in) in length.

Distribution A genus from Ordovician strata worldwide. The specimen illustrated is from New York, USA.

Ampyx

This specimen is typical of a fossil trilobite in that it is beginning to disarticulate. The cephalon is almost separated from the thorax. There are six thoracic segments and the cephalon is the same size as the pygidium, which tapers to a point. In complete specimens there is a long spine projecting from the glabella, only a small part of which is preserved on the specimen illustrated. The glabella extends beyond the border of the cephalon.

Size A small trilobite, growing up to 15mm (0.6in) in length.
Distribution This genus is from the Middle Ordovician rocks of North America and Europe.

Onnia

Onnia is characterized by a very large cephalon, the only part preserved in the specimen illustrated. This has a perforated border and the glabella is prominent, rounded and without eyes. In complete specimens there are long, thin genal spines. The short thorax has 5-7 segments. The pygidium is small and triangular. It has been suggested that the perforated border of the cephalon may have been used for detecting the movement of water currents.

Size A genus of small trilobites growing up to 20mm (0.8in) in length.

Distribution This trilobite is found in rocks of Middle and Upper Ordovician age in Europe, north Africa and South America. The specimen shown is from Wales.

Dalmanites

This genus has 12-16 thoracic segments, and a large cephalon with a furrowed glabella that bulges forward. There are large crescentric eyes. The pygidium is triangular and tapers to a long spine, only a small part of which is present in the specimen illustrated. There are also long genal spines from the cephalon, and a short frontal spine.

Size This trilobite reached up to 80mm (3.2in) in length.

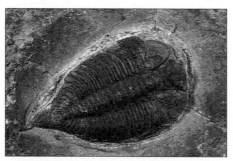

Distribution A genus from the Silurian and Devonian rocks of the CIS, North America, Australia and Europe. The specimen shown is from Shropshire, UK.

Trimerus

This genus is characterized by a very wide thoracic axis and only indistinct longitudinal lobes. The pygidium is large and of more usual trilobite construction, with a definite axial lobe. It is triangular and tapers to a narrow point. The cephalon is without borders. The smoothness of the exoskeleton and lack of eyes has led to the suggestion that this trilobite may have burrowed in the mud on the sea-bed.

Size *Trimerus* grew to 200mm (8in) in length.

Distribution This trilobite is found in rocks of Silurian and Devonian age worldwide. The specimen illustrated is from Shropshire, UK.

Encrinurus

The photograph shows the fossil *(left)* and the mould it has made in the soft sea-floor mud *(right)*. This genus can be recognized by the characteristic tuberculation (many small raised lumps) on the cephalon and pygidium. The eyes were on small stalks, rarely preserved in fossils because they were of very delicate structure. There are 12 thoracic segments. The thorax lacks tuberculation, and the triangular pygidium tapers to a sharp point. Trilobites with their eyes on stalks are often interpreted as living in the mud on the sea-bed.

Size A genus that grew to 80mm (3.2in) in length.
Distribution This trilobite is from strata of Ordovician to Devonian age worldwide.

Calymene

Two specimens of this common genus are shown, one of which is characteristically enrolled. This feature of many trilobites has been attributed to various functions. Modern small arthropods, such as the wood-louse (pillbug), enroll defensively. It has been argued that trilobites may have done it for this reason, or even at times of food shortage. This trilobite has 12 thoracic segments. The cephalon, which is the same size as the pygidium, has a large glabella. There are deep grooves and large eyes beside the glabella. The pygidium is triangular and has six segments.

Size A genus that grew to 100mm (4in) in length.

Distribution This trilobite is found in Silurian and Devonian rocks in North America, South America, Australia and Europe. Both specimens are from Shropshire, UK.

Bumastus

This genus is characterized by having a narrow thorax with 10 segments, and a large, almost unornamented pygidium and cephalon. Both these features are rounded and smooth. The glabella is indistinct. The eyes are well to the side of the glabella. Whole specimens, like the one shown, are rare in this genus and usually only the cephalon or pygidium is found. As

with many genera, this trilobite was able to enroll, possibly as a defensive adaptation. It is commonly found in limestone strata with a great variety of other fossils, such as brachiopods and corals.

Size *Bumastus* grew up to 100mm (4in) long.

Distribution This trilobite is found in strata of Silurian age in North America and Europe.

Leonaspis

This is a very spinose trilobite with spines developed from most of the thoracic segments and from the cephalon. The pygidium, which is very small and sub-rectangular, also has spines. There are prominent eyes beside the glabella. The thorax has 8-10 segments.

Size The genus grew to a maximum length of 20mm (0.8in).

Distribution *Leonaspis* is found in rocks of Silurian and Devonian age in North America, South America, Australia, Asia and Europe.

Phacops

This genus has characteristic tuberculation on the cephalon and the thoracic axis. The eyes are well developed, with compound lenses, and are occasionally well preserved, as in the specimen illustrated. There are no spines. The glabella is prominent. There are 11 segments in the thorax. Specimens of this genus are often found enrolled.

Size *Phacops* grew up to 60mm (2.4in) long.
Distribution A genus from Silurian and Devonian rocks in North America, north Africa and Europe. The specimen shown is from Morocco.

Acidaspis

This very spinose trilobite has 10 segments in the thorax, all of which have spines. The border of the small pygidium is spinose and tuberculate, the pygidium appearing almost like a small comb. The cephalon is fragmented in the specimen illustrated. When complete it has a tapering glabella and three pairs of lateral lobes.

Size *Acidaspis* is a small trilobite, reaching about 30mm (1.2in) long.
Distribution A genus from the Ordovician to Middle Devonian strata of North America and Europe.

Proetus

This genus has 8-10 thoracic segments and there is a pronounced furrow where the axis gives way to the pleurae. The well-segmented pygidium is semicircular. The glabella has only weak ornamentation and the eyes are large.

Size *Proetus* grew to about 30mm (1.2in) in length.

Distribution It is found worldwide in rocks ranging from Ordovician to Carboniferous in age. The specimen shown is from the Devonian strata of Germany.

Scutellum

The pygidium is illustrated here. It has a most interesting structure, with radiating ribs rather than the more usual trilobite segmentation. These ribs radiate from the point where the pygidium joins the thorax. Part of the outer shell has been broken off to reveal the delicate concentric markings on the underlying surface.

Size The pygidium shown is about 30mm (1.2in) long.

Distribution A genus from strata of Silurian to Devonian age worldwide. The specimen illustrated is from Prague, Czechoslovakia.

Eocyphinium

The group to which this trilobite belongs is often loosely referred to as *Phillipsia*. The pygidium is shown in the photograph, the remainder having been broken off before preservation. This part of the trilobite is well segmented and coarsely pustulate. The cephalon is sub-triangular and the thorax has 10 segments.

Size
The pygidium shown is 15mm (0.6in) long.
Distribution
A trilobite from the Lower Carboniferous strata of Europe.

Other arthropods

As well as trilobites, many other arthropods are preserved in the fossil record: Creatures such as crabs, lobsters, eurypterids and even delicate insects are not uncommon. Many insects are preserved in amber, which is fossilized resin. These insects became stuck in the fragrant resin seeping from pine trees and when the resin hardened to amber they were fossilized.

Pterygotus

Pterygotus

This creature belongs to the order Eurypterida. They inhabited marine and brackish water, and were scorpion-like creatures. The body is segmented and equipped with large, strong claws, probably used for holding prey. *Pterygotus* had large eyes and paddle-shaped limbs, both of which further indicate their active and predatory lifestyle. A whole specimen and a single claw are shown.

Size These fierce predators grew to about 2 metres (78in) in length. Specimens of about 200mm (8in), like the one shown, are more common.

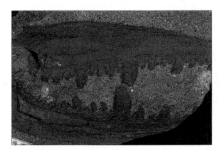

Distribution They are found in rocks of Upper Ordovician to Devonian age in North and South America, Europe, Asia and Australia. The specimens shown are from Scotland.

Euphorberia

This specimen is preserved in an ironstone nodule, both halves of which are shown. The creature belongs to the Chilopoda, a class of mainly terrestrial arthropods related to modern millipedes and centipedes. Only rarely are such land-living arthropods fossilized because of the lower chance of their being covered with sediment on land. *Euphorberia* inhabited the swamp forests of the Carboniferous period. The slender body has a segmented thorax and appendages.

Size A genus that grew to about 80mm (3.2in) long.

Distribution This arthropod is found in the Upper Carboniferous rocks of North America and Europe. The specimen illustrated is from Staffordshire, UK.

Euproops

Like *Euphorberia*, this specimen is preserved in an iron-stone nodule. *Euproops* is related to modern horse-shoe crabs, and resembles them in general appearance. It also has many features reminiscent of the trilobites, having a head-shield and segmented thorax. There are large genal spines extending from the head-shield, and the pleurae also carry spines, giving the thoracic margin a 'webbed' appearance.

Size A genus that grew to about 40mm (1.6in) in length.

Distribution
Euproops is found in rocks of Upper Carboniferous and Permian age in North America and Europe. The specimen illustrated is from North Staffordshire, UK.

Mesolimulus

This arthropod is characterized by a large dorsal head-shield, spinose thorax and a long, pointed tail spine. The thorax has a central glabella with two simple eyes in front and large compound eyes on either side. There are five pairs of legs. Many related modern genera live off the Atlantic coast of North America, in the mangrove swamps of south-east Asia and in the Indian Ocean. They feed on vegetation and crustaceans, and swim with the carapace below and the legs above. The fossil forms probably had a similar lifestyle.

Size The genus grows to about 250mm (10in) in length.

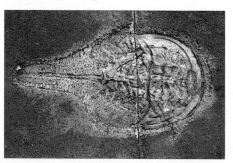

Distribution
It is found in Mesozoic rocks in Europe.

Glyphea

This animal is a member of the Decapoda, a group of crustaceans, and is related to lobsters and shrimps. It had five pairs of limbs, which are rarely preserved as fossils. There is a carapace with a rough, granulose surface, which protected the body. The head has appendages and eyes. Fossils of this arthropod have been found associated with the trace fossil *Thalassinoides* (see p. 182), and it is thought that *Glyphea* may have constructed these now fossilized burrows.

Size A small arthropod that grew to about 45mm (1.8in) long.
Distribution The genus is found in rocks of Triassic to Cretaceous age in North America, Europe, Greenland, East Africa and Australia. The specimen illustrated is from North Yorkshire, UK.

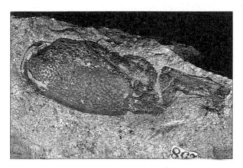

Euestheria

This small, shelled arthropod, which superficially resembles a mollusc, belongs to the class Branchiopoda, sub-phylum Crustacea. The bivalved carapaces shown here have concentric growth lines left by ecdysis (moulting).

Size The genus grew to about 10mm (0.4in) in length.
Distribution It is found in rocks of Triassic and Jurassic age worldwide.

Archaeogeryon

Fossils of crabs are not uncommon in shallow-water marine strata. They resemble modern crabs and the hard carapace, with its rough surface of many small, raised markings, is usually well preserved. Sometimes this part of the animal is crushed and only the limbs survive. The specimen shown is preserved in a concretion.

Size This genus grew to about 100mm (4in) in width.
Distribution Found in rocks of Tertiary age worldwide. This specimen is from the Miocene strata of South America.

Libellula

This delicate fossil is of a dragonfly larva preserved in very fine-grained limestone. Such organisms can usually only become fossilized when the depositional conditions are tranquil and when rapid burial in soft lime mud occurs. The larval stage of a dragonfly is aquatic, so preservation of this stage of the insect's development is more common than fossilization of the adult. The illustration shows the typical features of a dragonfly larva, including the legs, segmented thorax and small head.

Size The specimen illustrated is 15mm (0.6in) long.
Distribution The order Odonata (dragonflies) ranges from Triassic to Recent in age. The specimen shown is from Miocene rocks at Piedmont, Italy.

Hoploparia

This fossil lobster has many features similar to its modern relatives. There is a segmented shell with slender, pointed limbs, best seen in the larger specimen. Fossilized lobsters are not infrequent in shallow marine strata because the hard shell and appendages are durable. Such creatures are often preserved in clay or iron-rich concretions, as are the two specimens shown.

Size The larger specimen is 60mm (2.4in) long, but is of an incomplete lobster. The smaller, more typical, fragmented specimen is 40mm (1.6in) long.

Distribution This genus is found in rocks of Tertiary age worldwide.

Mollusca

Creatures belonging to this diverse phylum first appear in the fossil record in strata of Cambrian age. It is believed that their ancestors in the Pre-Cambrian were probably segmented and worm-like, or not unlike the modern Monoplacophora, which have a low rounded shell with the soft organs inside, and a fleshy foot below. The phylum contains a great variety of creatures; many of the groups have a soft body enclosed in the mantle, an internal or external shell, and a foot. When the total number of species is counted, the Mollusca are second to the Arthropoda at the present time. There are a number of classes within the phylum, many of which are shelled and have a mantle from which the shell is secreted. These include the Bivalvia, molluscs with two, often similar shells, such as the cockles, mussels and oysters; the Cephalopoda, a class containing squids, octopus, cuttle, nautilus and extinct ammonites; and the Gastropoda, which contains the snails and slugs. All three classes are very well represented as fossils, and their evolution is well documented. Two less well-known classes are the Scaphopoda (tusk-shells) and the Amphineura (chitons).

The phylum includes creatures that live in the sea, fresh and brackish water, others which inhabit dry land, and some molluscs that even climb trees.

Fossil molluscs are of great interest and use to the palaeontologist. The Ammonoidea, including goniatites, ceratites and ammonites, are a classic example of fossils that are useful in relative dating and correlation of the strata in which they are found. Other molluscs, especially the Bivalvia, are of use in reconstructing the depositional environment of rocks. This is largely because many bivalve molluscs are very particular as to water depth, sea-floor material and salinity, and modern molluscs of similar type can be compared with fossils.

Scaphopoda (Tusk shells)

This class is characterized by a thin, tapering shell, which is tubular and open at both ends. Modern genera live in sand on the sea bed, with the tapering end protruding into the water. Sea water is sucked into and expelled from this end of the shell. From the other end project the foot and numerous very thin, ciliated arms. Other soft parts include a head with radula (jaws) and feeding tentacles. Modern species feed on minute, single-celled *Foraminifera*. They are not very common as fossils, and about a thousand species are alive today.

Dentalium

Three species of this genus of scaphopod are illustrated.
Dentalium is reasonably well known as a fossil, and is
characterized by longitudinal ribs on its hollow, tube-shaped
shell. The dark-coloured specimen is *Dentalium priseum*, from
the Carboniferous strata of southern Scotland. In the centre is
Dentalium sexangulare, from rocks of Miocene age in Tuscany,
Italy. The thin, slightly curved, tusk-like shells are of
Dentalium striatum from Eocene strata in Hampshire, UK.
Size *Dentalium* is about 60mm (2.4in) long.
Distribution It is found in rocks of Silurian to Pleistocene age
worldwide.

Bivalvia (Bivalves)

Also known as the Pelecypoda and Lamellibranchia, the class
Bivalvia is characterized by two valves making up the shell,
which is usually symmetrical, with the plane of symmetry
passing between the valves. The scallops, mussels, oysters,
clams and tellins are well-known bivalves. They first appear in
rocks of Cambrian age and are common today. The two valves
are held together and opened by a combination of two muscles
(one in some genera) and a horny ligament. The chitinous
ligament pulls the valves apart slightly when the muscles relax.
Near the beak or umbo of the shell, on the inside, there is an
arrangement of projections (teeth), and corresponding hollows
(sockets) in the other valve, which act as the hinging
mechanism.

The actual position and size of the adductor muscles can be
estimated in dead shells and in fossils by studying the muscle
scars. These are rounded impressions on the inside of the
shell, often one at the anterior and another at the posterior end

(the end away from which the umbones often point and the part of the shell which in many genera is elongated). When two adductor muscles are present they are commonly joined by a thin line, the pallial line, which marks the margin of the attachment of the mantle to the shell. The mantle is rather like an interior fleshy envelope which contains the animal's soft parts. When the pallial line has an indentation (the pallial sinus), this indicates that the creature was a burrower, as the sinus marks the position of the retractor muscles needed to pull the large siphons into the shell. The inhalent siphon is used for feeding. Microscopic organisms are sucked into the shell, where they are trapped on mucous-covered gills and passed to the mouth. The exhalent siphon removes waste matter.

Bivalves have become adapted to many environments, both marine and freshwater. Some, such as the oysters, are permanently attached to the sea-bed, while others, like *Mya*, are burrowers. By flapping their valves together with a single large muscle, pectens can swim in the water column, and many bivalves move slowly across the sea-bed by pushing themselves along with a tough, fleshy, tongue-like foot. This is a very common class of molluscs in the fossil record, and today there are over 10,000 living species. They are usually quite small – about 10-100mm (0.4in-4in) in diameter – but there are enormous bivalves which are 1.5 metres (5ft) across.

Posidonia

A genus with flattened valves and an almost circular outline. The dorsal margin of the shell is straight. There are well-formed growth lines raised from the shell surface. The umbones point anteriorly, and there is slight posterior elongation of the shell. The valves are very thin and can have narrow ribs. Inside the shell there is a single muscle scar.
Size This genus reached about 35mm (1.4in) in diameter.

Distribution It is found worldwide in rocks of Carboniferous to Jurassic age. The specimen shown is from the Carboniferous rocks of Belgium.

Dunbarella

This is a thin-shelled genus with a very pointed umbo and delicate radiating ribs crossing the shell. The concentric growth lines are less pronounced. The overall shape is sub-triangular and not unlike Pecten (see p. 109) in general appearance. This genus is often preserved on bedding planes of dark shale with other marine creatures such as goniatites.

Size This bivalve grew to about 40mm (1.6in) in diameter.
Distribution *Dunbarella* is from Carboniferous strata in North America and Europe.

Carbonicola

A genus of non-marine bivalves, *Carbonicola* is used along with other molluscs to correlate the strata that contain coal seams. It has a small- to medium-sized shell with similar valves, which have a slight posterior elongation. The growth lines are the main shell ornamentation and the umbo faces anteriorly. This genus was not anchored to the substrate; it moved through the mud with its fleshy foot.
Size A genus of up to 60mm (2.4in) in length.
Distribution It is found in strata of Upper Carboniferous age in Europe and the CIS.

Anthraconauta

This illustration shows masses of shells of this elongate bivalve on a shale bedding plane. The main shell ornamentation is the concentric growth lines. A thin-shelled bivalve, *Anthraconauta* lived in non-marine conditions and, along with genera like *Carbonicola*, is used for sub-dividing and correlating coal-bearing strata of Carboniferous age.

Size This genus grew to about 50mm (2in) in length.
Distribution It is found in rocks of Carboniferous and Permian age in western Europe and the CIS.

Schizodus

A smooth-shelled genus, which is shown here as internal casts, the valves having been removed by fluids circulating through the sediment in which they were buried. The fossils are made of the sediment which infilled the empty valves. Details such as the ribs and growth lines can be seen.
Size This genus grew to about 50mm (2in) in length.
Distribution *Schizodus* is found in strata of Carboniferous and Permian age worldwide.

Hippopodium

A heavily built genus, with thick stout valves, *Hippopodium* has growth lines as its main shell ornamentation. These growth lines are slightly folded near the umbones. Ribs are usually absent. The shell is elongated posteriorly. It lived in marine conditions.

Size A genus that grew to about 80mm (3.2in) in length.

Distribution This bivalve is found in rocks of Lower Jurassic age in Europe and east Africa. The specimen illustrated is from Dorset, UK.

Cardinia

Cardinia has a sub-oval to sub-triangular shell outline. There are thick growth lines and indistinct ribs. The umbones point to the anterior edge of the shell. The two valves are similar, being thick and strong, and adapted to living in shallow marine conditions.

Size This genus is of average size for a bivalve mollusc. It grew to a maximum length of about 200mm (8in).

Distribution It is found in rocks of Upper Triassic and Lower Jurassic age with a worldwide distribution. It is commonly

found in sandstones, shales and mudstones, with a variety of fossils such as ammonites and other bivalves.

Oxytoma

A genus with a sub-rounded shell, the valves of which are different, one being more convex than the other. There are wings beside the umbones and, as in the specimen illustrated, there may be a large, extended spine from this part of the shell. There are different orders of ribs, with a few very strong ribs and finer ones in between. Growth lines are indistinct, and between the ribs the shell is nearly smooth.

Size This bivalve grew to about 60mm (2.4in) in length.
Distribution It is found in rocks of Upper Triassic to Upper Cretaceous age worldwide.

Nuculana

This small bivalve has a sub-triangular outline and umbones pointing anteriorly. The valves are elongated posteriorly. The shell is ornamented with growth lines. This genus is frequently found in the same dark shale strata as other bivalves and ammonites.
Size *Nuculana* grows to about 20mm (0.8in).
Distribution The genus is found worldwide in rocks of Triassic to Recent age.

Lopha

This is a genus of oysters characterized by very strong valves, and therefore capable of withstanding the turbulent conditions of shallow seas. There are many stout ribs crossing the shell. Two valves are shown, stuck together during fossilization. The one on the left shows the external ornamentation, while the one on the right illustrates the internal structure, with a large muscle scar and single hinge tooth. One of the valves is convex, the other concave. This genus lived anchored to the sea-bed.

Size *Lopha* grew to about 120mm (4.8in) in length. **Distribution** The genus is found in rocks of Triassic to Cretaceous age worldwide.

Chlamys

This bivalve has unequally convex valves and very pronounced ears near the umbo. One of these ears is usually much larger than the other, as in the specimen illustrated. There are many radiating ribs and the shell may be spinose. Some species lived anchored to the sea-floor by a mass of threads (byssus), while others were able to swim. The hinge line is elongated and straight.

Size A bivalve that grows to about 100mm (4in) in length. **Distribution** It is found in strata of Triassic to Recent age worldwide.

Plagistoma

This genus is relatively smooth-shelled, with faint growth lines as the main ornamentation. There are also very thin ribs radiating from the umbo. The posterior of the shell is rounded and there is an overall sub-triangular outline. On the anterior side of the shell near the umbo is a small winged extension.

Size A medium-sized bivalve which grew to about 120mm (4.8in) in diameter.
Distribution It is found in rocks of Triassic to Cretaceous age worldwide.

Exogyra

A genus of oyster which is very inequivalved and has developed spirally, with the umbones coiled posteriorly. There are rounded shell margins with radial ribbing. There may also be scales and spines on the valves. The shell margin is denticulate. A deep ridge divides the shell into two parts. During life one valve was attached to the sea-bed.

Size This oyster grew to a maximum length of about 200mm (8in).
Distribution A genus from the Cretaceous rocks of Europe.

Myophorella

This is a strikingly ornamented bivalve of sub-triangular shape. It has very thick valves, with rows of heavy tubercles following the positions which growth lines would take. The umbones point inward, and the valves have one straight edge and one curved edge. This genus lived in shallow water and burrowed in the sea-bed.

Size It grew to about 100mm (4in) in length.
Distribution A bivalve mollusc from rocks of Jurassic and Cretaceous age worldwide.

Camptonectes

This bivalve has one valve more convex than the other. It is a beautiful shell with a very rounded outline. There are pointed umbones with ears (wings) on either side. The shell surface ornamentation consists of fine lines and punctations which may be divergent or curved.

Size A large bivalve growing to about 200mm (8in) in diameter.
Distribution This genus is from rocks of Lower Jurassic to Upper Cretaceous age worldwide.

Pinna

A genus with a wedge-shaped or elongated shell, *Pinna* is seen
here preserved as internal calcareous casts. There are pointed
umbones and the shell surface is ornamented with radiating
ribs and marginal undulations. It is a thin-shelled bivalve with
a slight ridge down the long axis of the valves. *Pinna* lived half-
buried in the sea-floor sediment, anchored by byssal threads.
The posterior end of the shell protruded. It is found in a
variety of rocks, including limestones and shales, with many
other fossils. These include brachiopods, cephalopods and

other bivalves.
Size A large
genus growing to
400mm (16in)
maximum length.
Distribution It
is found in rocks
of Lower
Carboniferous to
Recent age
worldwide.

Pseudomytiloides

This is a thin-shelled genus with a rounded to sub-triangular
shell. There are very pointed umbones, and the shell surface
is ornamented with numerous ridges following the general
pattern of growth lines. This bivalve is often preserved in dark
shales and replaced with pyrite, as in the specimen illustrated.
It often occurs with fossil ammonites, such as *Dactylioceras*,
and other bivalve molluscs, which may also be replaced with
pyrite.

Size It grew to
bout 40mm
(1.6in) in length.
Distribution A
genus from the
Lower Jurassic
rocks of Europe
and Asia.

Laevitrigonia

This specimen shows preservation as an internal cast, with lime mud having infilled the shell and then the shell itself having been removed, possibly by chemical action. Much detail can still be seen of the inside of the valves, including the pallial line and the muscle scars. The valves have a definite posterior elongation, and the umbo leans anteriorly.

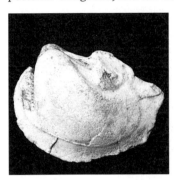

Size The specimen is typical at 50mm (2in) in length.
Distribution *Laevitrigonia* is found in Jurassic rocks in Europe, Asia, the Middle East and east Africa. The specimen illustrated is from southern England.

Pseudopecten

A genus with a sub-triangular shell outline, this bivalve has strong, square-sectioned ribs radiating from the pointed umbones. There are also growth lines ornamenting the shell. On the inside of each valve is one large muscle scar. *Pseudopecten* belongs to a group of bivalves which, by flapping their valves together, are able to swim.
Size This bivalve grew to about 200mm (8in) in diameter.
Distribution It is found in rocks of Jurassic age in Europe, South America and the East Indies. The specimen illustrated, a bedding plane crowded with disarticulated valves, is from the Lower Jurassic of North Yorkshire, UK.

Gryphaea

This genus has a number of different species, which are commonly found as fossils. They are oysters and have developed various adaptations and shell shapes for their sedentary mode of life on the sea-bed. *Gryphaea arcuata* has a very inequivalve shell. One valve is large and curved with a hooked umbo, while the other is small and concave or flat. This smaller valve fits inside the larger one and is uppermost in the illustration. The larger valve is very thick and has stout growth lines as ornamentation. There is also a radial groove, or sulcus, on the posterior side of the larger valve. The other species shown is *Gryphaea giganteum*. This oyster has a much wider, flatter shell than *G. arcuata*. The shell has a rounded outline, with one very convex and one concave valve. The heavy, thick shell of this species is ornamented with growth lines.

Size *Gryphaea arcuata* grew to about 160mm (6.4in) in length. *G. giganteum* is somewhat larger, reaching about 200mm (8in) in diameter. **Distribution** The genus *Gryphaea* is found in rocks of Upper Triassic to Upper Jurassic age worldwide.

Modiolus

This is the ancestor and close relative of the modern mussel shell, well known as a bivalve of shallow marine habitats. *Modiolus* is a common fossil bivalve genus in marine strata. It has a prominent posterior elongation of the shell, with concentric growth lines as the main ornamentation. The shell is thin and the umbones are small and point anteriorly.

Size This genus grows to a maximum length of about 100mm (4in).
Distribution It is found worldwide in rocks from Devonian to Recent in age.

Pholadomya

The genus has a very elongate shell with a pronounced posterior gape. This feature allows the siphons to extend from the shell while it is in a burrow in the sea-bed sediment where the valves are unable to open. The pallial line has a pronounced sinus, another characteristic related to a burrowing mode of life. Such features are found in modern species of the genus *Mya*. The valves are ornamented with ribs and growth lines.

Size This bivalve grows to about 120mm (4.8in) in length.
Distribution *Pholadomya* is found in rocks of Triassic to Recent age worldwide. The specimen illustrated is from Gloucestershire, UK.

Inoceramus

This genus of bivalve mollusc has broad ridges running across the valves almost at right angles to the direction of the numerous growth lines. The shell is made up of convex valves and has a sub-oval outline. The specimen illustrated has some shell remaining, which shows as a whitish film on the fossil.

Size A bivalve that grew to about 120mm (4.8in) in length.
Distribution It is found in rocks of Jurassic and Cretaceous age worldwide.

Spondylus

This shell has beautifully symmetrical valves, with stout, almost square-sectioned ribs radiating from the umbones. The umbo on each valve is small and pointed, and growth lines cover the shell surface. Though rare in fossils, delicate spines may extend from the shell. The specimen shown is typical in that only the stumps of these remain. The spines probably helped to secure the animal in the soft sea-bed mud.

Size A genus which grows to about 120mm (4.8in) in length.
Distribution It is found in strata of Jurassic to Recent age worldwide.

Venericardia

A genus well suited to living in shallow, possibly turbulent waters, *Venericardia* has a massive, thick shell with a very strong hinge mechanism. There are deep muscle scars on the inside of the valves. The ribs are wide and radiating, and sub-quadrate in section. Growth lines are less prominent. The margins of the valves are crenulated.

Size A large shell, growing to about 150mm (6in) in diameter.
Distribution This genus is found in rocks ranging from Palaeocene to Eocene in age in North America, Africa and Europe.

Hippurites

A bizarre bivalve that has one tube-like valve and the other attached as an operculum (lid). The outside of the larger valve is very rough and wrinkled, with ridges and furrows running around it. The genus lived attached to the sea-floor, with the operculum uppermost, looking not unlike a coral.
Size This bivalve grew to a maximum diameter of 120mm (4.8in).

Distribution It is found in rocks of Upper Cretaceous age in Europe, north Africa and south-east Asia.

Eoradiolites

This genus is similar to *Hippurites* in the strange shape of its shell. One valve is tube-like and the other smaller valve is attached as a lid. It can be cone-shaped. The larger valve is ornamented with deep grooves and wavy ridges. It was firmly anchored to the sea-bed when alive.

Size It grew to a diameter of about 50mm (2in).
Distribution *Eoradiolites* is found in rocks of Cretaceous age in North America, Europe and Asia. The specimen illustrated is from Iowa, USA.

Glycimeris

This bivalve has thick, convex valves with small, beaked umbones. On the inside of each valve there are large muscle scars joined by a simple pallial line. The shell has two rows of slanting hinge-teeth for holding the valves together. These features are evident in the larger of the two specimens shown. The valves are of equal size and almost circular in outline. The ornamentation on the outside of the shell consists of growth lines and thin radiating ribs.
Size This genus grows to about 60mm (2.4in) in diameter.

Distribution It is found in rocks of Cretaceous to Recent age worldwide.

Teredo

This bivalve genus is rather different from many in that it burrows into wood. The animal is small and tube-like. The specimen shows many such animals in their life position. Often the burrows are preserved as trace fossils, and the shell is missing or present at one end of the burrow.

Size The tubes shown are about 9mm (0.36in) in diameter.
Distribution *Teredo* is found in strata of Eocene to Recent age worldwide. The specimen illustrated is from the Eocene rocks of southern England.

Pecten

A bivalve with an almost circular shell outline, the valves having great symmetry with each other. However, one valve is convex or flat and the other is concave. Two definite ears, with growth lines, are present on either side of the umbo, which is rounded. Thick ribs, with narrow grooves between them, and numerous growth lines ornament the shell. Species of this genus were able to swim by flapping their valves together.

Size *Pecten* grows up to 80mm (3.2in) in diameter.
Distribution The genus is found in strata of Eocene to Recent age worldwide.

Gastropoda (Gastropods)

This class of mollusc is characterized by a shell which is usually coiled in an upward spiral. Gastropods are a very common group, being the most abundant molluscs. They have been recorded in strata from Cambrian times onwards and are the well-known snails and slugs of today. Although the shell is usually spirally coiled, some forms have a simple cone-shaped shell, while in other genera the shell is absent. The body of a gastropod is different from that of other molluscs in that it has been twisted (a process called torsion) early in its life. This causes the nervous system to adopt a figure-of-eight shape, and the mantle cavity is rotated anticlockwise. Modern gastropods have become adapted to all manner of environments. They live on dry land and in marine and freshwater habitats. Some even climb trees.

Poleumita

This gastropod is coiled, with a flattened upper shell surface. There is a pronounced ridge on the centre of the whorls. Numerous small spines can be present as ornamentation, and the shell surface is covered with thin, radiating lamellae. The aperture is more commonly angular than rounded.

Size A genus which grew to about 60mm (2.4in) in diameter.
Distribution It is from rocks of Silurian age in North America and Europe. The specimen shown is from Shropshire, UK.

Tentaculites

This genus is commonly found preserved in Palaeozoic strata, but it has uncertain affinities. It is usually considered to be in the group Pteropoda, which also contains modern pelagic gastropods. The shell is small and cone-shaped, and has a circular cross-section. Some are internally divided by septa. As seen in the specimens illustrated, which are fossilized on a bedding plane with brachiopods, the shell of *Tentaculites* has thick ribs around it.

Size It grew to about 12mm (0.5in) in length.
Distribution This fossil is found in strata of Silurian to Devonian age worldwide.

Straparollus

This gastropod has a characteristically coiled shell, but can vary in its coiling from having a high spiral shape to being quite flat. The shell surface is smooth but, as clearly seen in the specimen illustrated, there are numerous thin ribs crossing the whorls. A slight ridge runs down the centre of each whorl.
Size A gastropod that grew to about 50mm (2in) in diameter.

Distribution It is found in rocks of Silurian to Permian age worldwide. The specimen shown is from the Carboniferous rocks of Derbyshire, UK.

Bellerophon

This genus has a large, rounded shell with a prominent keel around the centre of each whorl. There are numerous ribs crossing the shell, which curve slightly as they cross the keel. The shell is heavily built and has strong bilateral symmetry. There is a flared aperture with a deep slit on the front margin and a narrow convex border.

Size *Bellerophon* grew to about 80mm (3.2in) in diameter.
Distribution This gastropod is found in rocks of Silurian to Triassic age worldwide.

Mourlonia

A gastropod with a typical pointed, spire-shaped shell, this genus has whorls that are ornamented with very thin, spirally arranged ribs. The apex of the shell is rounded. As the whorls widen towards the shell aperture, they become flatter. There is a narrow suture between the whorls.

Size The genus reached to 40mm (1.6in) in diameter.
Distribution *Mourlonia* is found in strata of Ordovician to Permian age worldwide.

Bourguetia

This sea snail has a large, heavy shell, which tapers to a blunt apex. The whorls are generally smooth, but can be ornamented with growth lines. The sutures (the grooves between the whorls) are deeply set. The specimen illustrated appears to have numerous small, rounded markings on its shell. These are ooliths, the grains of oolitic limestone in which it is preserved.

Size A moderately large gastropod, growing to about 100mm (4in) in length.

Distribution The genus is found in the Middle and Upper Jurassic of Europe. The specimen illustrated is from North Yorkshire, UK.

Pleurotomaria

Coiling in a low spiral, the whorls gradually increase in size towards the aperture. This is large and flared, and has a long slit on its upper margin. The ornamentation is clearly visible in the illustration and includes growth lines, tubercles and

spirally arranged bands. The suture is deep.

Size The shell grew to a maximum height of about 120mm (4.8in).

Distribution This genus is from rocks of Jurassic and Cretaceous age worldwide.

Pseudomelania

A gastropod with an elongated, multi-coiled shell. The apex is pointed and the suture deeply set. A ridge is present on each whorl. The specimens illustrated are typical in having been preserved as internal moulds, with none of the original shell remaining. They are simply the hardened lime mud which infilled the empty, dead shells.

Size This genus grew to about 100mm (4in).
Distribution *Pseudomelania* is from rocks of Upper Jurassic age in Europe. The specimens seen here are from southern England.

Conotomaria

Conotomaria has a pronounced, cone-shaped shell. The whorls are only faintly distinguished from each other by a moderately deep suture. The shell has a flat base. The ornamentation consists of many encircling spiral lines and low ridges. The specimen shown is an internal cast. This genus lived and crawled on the sea-bed, and is commonly found with a variety of other fossils, including bivalve molluscs and ammonites.

Size *Conotomaria* grew to a maximum height of about 150mm (6in).
Distribution This genus is from Middle Jurassic to Palaeocene rocks worldwide.

Sycostoma

A beautifully constructed shell, which has a large body whorl and other whorls forming a conical structure with a rounded apex. There are ribs on the shell surface, and slight ridges follow the sutures, which separate the whorls from each other. The aperture is slightly flared.

Size *Sycostoma* grew to a maximum height of about 70mm (2.8in).

Distribution
The genus is found in strata of Upper Cretaceous to Oligocene age worldwide.

Cerithium

This is a slender, tapering, cone-shaped genus constructed of numerous small whorls. There is a small aperture, and each whorl has a definite ridge ornamented with small spines and tubercles. There are spiral growth lines. The specimens shown are preserved in clay, along with the impressions of others.

Size The shell grows to about 30mm (1.2in) in length.

Distribution
This genus is found in rocks of Upper Cretaceous to Recent age worldwide. It is especially common in the Paris Basin, France, and in Texas, USA.

Natica

A genus of gastropod with a thick, smooth, globular shell of almost hemispherical shape. The apex is short and flattened. Thin sutures separate the whorls. Ornamentation consists of faint, curved striae crossing the shell. In life the aperture had an operculum (lid), which is often missing in fossils. The body whorl is very large compared with the other whorls. This genus is a predator and drills holes into other shellfish.

Size *Natica* grows to about 30mm (1.2in) in height.

Distribution The shell is found in strata ranging in age from Cretaceous to Recent worldwide. The specimen shown is from the Eocene of Marne, France.

Ancilla

A smooth-shelled, tapering gastropod with thin sutures and a large aperture. The body whorl is far bigger than the others, which end in a sharp apex. There is a broad siphonal notch and the shell is ornamented with delicate growth lines. If preservation is exceptionally good, the glossy shell surface remains. In rocks of Tertiary age, this genus occurs with a variety of other gastropod fossils.

Size The genus grows to about 50mm (2.0in) in length.
Distribution *Ancilla* is found in strata of Upper Cretaceous to Recent age worldwide.

Ficus

This gastropod has a pear-shaped shell, the biggest whorl of which (the body chamber) covers most of the other whorls to such an extent that only the tapering, pointed apex projects. The aperture is very large and tapers to a narrow base. The shell is ornamented with reticulate criss-crossing sculptures.
Size The genus reaches a maximum length of about 100mm (4in). This genus lived in shallow marine conditions, with a

wide variety of other gastropods.
Distribution *Ficus* is found in strata of Palaeocene to Recent age worldwide.

Rimella

A genus of gastropod with a small but beautifully formed shell, which has a tapering spire and a canal reaching from the aperture almost to the apex. The shell is variously ornamented with delicately curved ribs and striations.
Size This gastropod reaches a maximum length of about 30mm (1.2in).
Distribution It is found in strata of Upper Cretaceous to Recent age worldwide.

Voluta

This gastropod has a stout shell, with a large body chamber whose strong ridges run to the narrow base. The aperture is narrow and slender. The smaller whorls end in a conical apex ornamented with spines and nodes. Growth lines also cover the shell surface. Two specimens are shown here to illustrate the shell structure and the aperture. The generic name *Voluta* has been much refined recently, and many genera that used to have this name are now in the genus *Athleta*.

Size It grows to a maximum length of 120mm (4.8in). **Distribution** *Voluta* is found in strata of Eocene to Recent age worldwide. The specimens shown are from Hampshire, UK.

Volutospina

A shell which closely resembles *Voluta*. The main difference is in the aperture ornamentation. There are several weak folds and one major fold on the columella in *Volutospina*, whereas *Voluta* has four or five folds. The ornamentation of *Volutospina* is of spiral ridges and less prominent growth lines. A very characteristic feature is the series of pointed nodes along the whorl shoulders.

Size This gastropod is of average size and grows to a maximum length of about 120mm (4.8in).

Distribution This genus is found in rocks of Upper Cretaceous to Recent age worldwide.

Conus

The shell is biconical and tapers to a point at both ends. There is a large body whorl with a long, narrow aperture. The other whorls taper pyramidally and have ridges running round them. The shell is also ornamented with growth lines and nodes, which give it a rough surface. *Conus* is often fossilized in great numbers, as shown in the photograph.

Size This genus grows to about 120mm (4.8in) long.

Distribution It is found in rocks ranging in age from Upper Cretaceous to Recent worldwide. The specimens shown are from Hampshire, UK.

Turritella

A screw shaped genus, with a characteristic long, slender shell. There are numerous whorls which have spiral ribbing. The whorls overlap only slightly, with deep sutures between them. This shell has a pointed apex. The body chamber, which has a simple aperture, is only slightly larger than the adjacent whorl. The modern species *Turritella communis* burrows into the sea-bed with the pointed end of the shell downwards, and the aperture just above the sediment surface.

Size This common genus grows to about 50mm (2in) in length.
Distribution *Turritella* is found in rocks of Cretaceous to Recent age worldwide.

Cornulina

This genus has a highly ornamented shell, which is covered with stout spines and tubercles. The body chamber is large compared with the other whorls. It has a flared aperture. The smaller whorls have an overall pyramidal shape and end in a sharp apex. As is common in fossils, many of the spines have been broken in this specimen.

Size A gastropod that grows to about 100mm (4in) in diameter.

Distribution It is found in rocks ranging in age from Miocene to Recent worldwide. The specimen illustrated is from Hampshire, UK.

Murex

This gastropod has a large, thick, highly ornamented shell. There are numerous long spines and tubercles, which tend to be in rows along the shell. Ribs and growth lines also ornament the shell. The body chamber is large and has an elongated aperture and long siphonal canal. The other smaller whorls give a pyramidal shape with a small, pointed apex.

Size *Murex* grows to about 100mm (4in) in length.
Distribution It is found in rocks of Miocene to Recent age worldwide.

Globularia

The name *Globularia* is very descriptive of this rounded, globose gastropod. The body chamber is large and inflated, and has a flared aperture. Other whorls form a flattened cone with a pointed apex. The shell is ornamented with many fine ridges, and the suture between the whorls is thin but moderately deep.

Size This gastropod grew to about 50mm (2in) in diameter.
Distribution It is found in strata ranging in age from Eocene to Oligocene worldwide.

Planorbis

This genus has a small, rounded shell, which is coiled almost in a flat plane and superficially resembles an ammonite shell. However, one side is concave and the other much flatter, whereas an ammonite shell is concave on both sides. This gastropod has a smooth surface with very faint growth lines. Between the whorls there is a deep suture. The aperture is ovoid. *Planorbis* lives in fresh water, and fossils of this genus are very useful in helping geologists to determine sedimentary environments.
Size The shell grows to a maximum diameter of about 30mm (1.2in).

Distribution *Planorbis* is found in strata of Oligocene to Recent age worldwide.

Hippochrenes

This gastropod is a marine snail with a very elegant shell. Its most striking feature is the broad, flat extension above the aperture, which is ornamented with growth lines and is as large as the rest of the shell. In fossils this feature is often broken off. The body chamber is large, with a sharply pointed siphonal canal. The other whorls are small and narrow, tapering through a long, tall, pyramidal spire to a sharp apex.
Size The genus grew to a maximum length of 150mm (6.0in).

Distribution It is found in rocks of Eocene age in Europe. The specimen illustrated is from southern England.

Turricula

This gastropod has a slender shell that tapers to a thin, pointed apex. The body whorl is large in comparison with the other whorls, and has a long, narrow aperture. It is more highly ornamented than the other parts of the shell, and has thick, closely spaced ribs. Each whorl has a row of tubercles around it, as well as thin striations.
Size *Turricula* grew to about 60mm (2.4in) in length.
Distribution It is found in strata of Eocene age worldwide.

Crucibulum

This mollusc has a cone-shaped shell, which is completely open. The shell is thick and pyramidal in outline, with an ornamentation of stout ribs that radiate from the apex. Wavy growth lines cross the shell. As can be seen from the specimens illustrated, there is a calcareous structure on the inside of the shell apex. This is thought to help the animal secure itself to the shell.

Size *Crucibulum* has a height of about 50mm (2in).
Distribution This shell is found in rocks of Miocene to Recent age in North America, Europe and the West Indies. The specimen illustrated is from Virginia, USA.

Cephalopoda (Cephalopods)

This group of molluscs is entirely marine. Many of them could swim freely by jet propulsion, while others probably lived a more sedentary life browsing on the sea-bed. Most cephalopods have a coiled shell, which is of interesting design Inside it is divided into chambers by walls called septa. The coiling is usually in a flat spiral, with the outermost whorl the largest, and the whorls (coils) becoming progressively smaller towards the centre. The body of the animal protruded from the shell aperture and occupied the first chamber (the body chamber), which took up much of the first whorl. The smaller internal chambers are the buoyancy chambers, allowing the animal to control its density and therefore its buoyancy. A thin tube, the siphuncle, passes from the body chamber through the buoyancy chambers. This may have allowed the regulation of fluids within the chambers. In the nautiloids the siphuncle is central in the whorls, but in the ammonoids it is marginal and near the ventral surface.

An important feature of externally shelled cephalopods is the series of suture lines which mark the position where the septa join the inner surface of the shell. These sutures are of varying complexity in different cephalopods. In the early ammonoids and nautiloids the sutures are simple in design, but they became much more complex in the Mesozoic ammonites. The sutures can be seen only when the outer surface of the shell has been removed. A complete ammonoid or nautiloid shell will have many sutures quite close together, but none on the undivided body chamber. If a shell has sutures all the way to its margin, it is an incomplete specimen with the body chamber absent. The body has a good nervous system, with tentacles and eyes. Indeed, these creatures are the most sophisticated of the invertebrates.

Many species today have an ink sac for shooting dark fluids as a defence mechanism. Fossils have been found with similar apparatus. The belemnites are cephalopods with straight internal shells and are closely related to modern squids. The cephalopods are first found in the fossil record in rocks of Cambrian age, and though they have been very diverse and numerous in the past, only a handful of genera of these delightful creatures survive today. The modern representatives include the octopus, squids, cuttles, nautiloids and argonauts.

Nautiloidea (Nautiloids)

A modern representative of this group, *Nautilus pompilius*, lives in tropical seas around Fiji, eastern Australia and Papua New Guinea. It has many similarities with fossil shells. However, some ancient nautiloids had orthocone (straight) shells and grew to great size, especially during the Lower Palaeozoic.

Cenoceras

This nautiloid has a typical involute shell structure, with the outer whorls covering the inner ones. The simple sutures cross the fossil and can be seen in the specimen illustrated because the outer shell is missing. When present, the shell has a criss-cross pattern of thin lines as ornamentation. The siphuncle is always near the centre of the whorls.

Size This large specimen is 140mm (5.6in) in diameter. **Distribution** A genus from Upper Triassic to Middle Jurassic strata worldwide.

Nautilus

Two specimens are illustrated, one of which has been cut to show the internal structure and photographed close up to show the detail. The shell of *Nautilus* has involute coiling, with the outer whorls obscuring much of the inner ones. The sutures, a good way of distinguishing nautiloids, are simple, curving forward slightly towards the shell aperture. The outer whorl is large and sub-rounded in cross-section. Shell ornamentation consists only of thin radiating lines. The sectioned specimen shows the internal septa dividing the shell into chambers, most of which have been infilled with pale calcite during fossilization. The siphuncle, a narrow tube passing through the chambers, can also be seen.

Size This genus grows to about 150mm (6in) in diameter.

Distribution A long-ranging genus, being found in rocks from Jurassic to Recent in age worldwide.

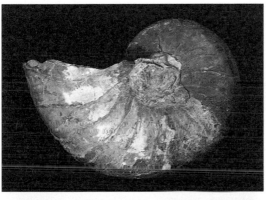

Orthoceras

This nautiloid has an almost circular shell cross-section and an overall tapering shape. The sectioned specimen clearly shows the septa dividing the shell into chambers, and the siphuncle. In some parts of the world masses of these shells are found, making what is called '*Orthoceras* limestone'. In these rocks (as at Lochkov, Czechoslovakia) the shells may be aligned by the direction of the sea-bed currents at the time of deposition. Thanks to the gas-filled buoyancy chambers, these and other cephalopod shells can drift great distances after the death of the organism. This produces a distribution wider than that in which the animal lived.

Size The genus could grow to a great size, up to several metres

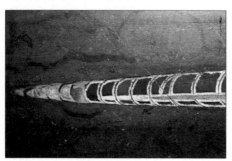

(many feet) in length.
Distribution It is found in strata of Lower Ordovician to Triassic age worldwide. The specimen illustrated is from the Silurian rocks of Shanghai,China.

Actinoceras

An orthocone nautiloid genus with a rather unusual internal structure, *Actinoceras* has a siphuncle that swells to a bulbous shape between the septa. The siphuncle is centrally positioned and has radiating branches. The specimen illustrated, which is somewhat broken, shows the characteristic chambered shell.

Size The thin, incomplete specimen shown here is 80mm (3.2in) long.

Distribution *Actinoceras* is found in rocks of Lower Ordovician to Carboniferous age worldwide. The specimen illustrated is from north-east Greenland.

Dawsonoceras

This genus of orthocone nautiloid is characterized by its stout shell, which tapers only slightly. The shell is ornamented with evenly spaced ribs, between which there are thin, wavy lines. The siphuncle is centrally placed. The cross-section of the shell is circular. In complete specimens there is an area of the shell at the wider end which is devoid of ribs.

Size
Dawsonoceras grew to about 750mm (30in) in length.
Distribution
This nautiloid is found in rocks of Silurian age in North America, Europe, Asia and Australia.

Gomphoceras

This is a strange-shaped nautiloid, with a shell that tapers to a point at one end and it has an overall egg-shaped appearance. Half the shell has broad ribs as ornamentation. A rounded ridge may be found at the end of the smooth part of the shell.
Size *Gomphoceras* grew to about 80mm (3.2in) in length.

Distribution
The genus is found in strata of Silurian age in Europe.

Ammonoidea (Ammonites)

This group of cephalopods first appears in the fossil record in rocks of Devonian age. They developed throughout the rest of the Palaeozoic era into the Mesozoic era, and died out towards the end of the Cretaceous period. The ammonoid shell is basically similar to that of *Nautilus,* but there are some important differences. The ammonoid siphuncle is normally placed ventrally, around the outer margin of each whorl, and the ammonoid suture line is often far more complex than the simple one of *Nautilus.* The nearest living relatives of the ammonoids are the squids and octopods; *Nautilus* is a far more distant relative.

Three broad groups of ammonoids, which are useful in helping to understand the differences in the sub-class, are the goniatites, which lived in the Devonian and Carboniferous periods; the ceratites, which were alive in the Permian and Triassic periods; and the ammonites, which flourished during Jurassic and Cretaceous times.

Like other shelled cephalopods, the ammonoid shell is divided into chambers separated by septa. The coils of the shell (whorls) are arranged in a plane spiral, with the umbilicus as the recessed centre. In some genera the whorls overlap so much that the innermost ones are more or less hidden. Such a shell is said to have involute coiling. The opposite of this, evolute coiling, is when the whorls hardly overlap and they can all be seen.

During their long history the ammonoids developed many forms differing from the usual small to medium-sized planospiral shell. Some grew to great size, like the Upper Jurassic *Titanites,* which is often nearly a metre (39in) in diameter, and the Upper Cretaceous *Parapuzosia,* which grew to 2.5 metres (97in) in diameter. Others, such as the Cretaceous *Scaphites* and *Nipponites,* uncoiled, and *Turrilites* from the Upper Cretaceous coiled in a spiral reminiscent of the gastropods.

This sub-class is of outstanding importance to stratigraphers (scientists who place the various strata into the correct sequence), because they have most of the main requirements needed to make them ideal zonal index fossils. A zone is the smallest manageable unit of relative geological time. A number of zones make up a time period, and periods are grouped into eras (see the time scale on p. 6). Many ammonoid species existed for only a very short time, but as they were free-swimming, or their shells drifted after death, they are widespread as fossils. The strata in which a given species is found were deposited over a short time-span. These strata form a zone named after the representative ammonoid and they can be correlated with strata in far-off places.

Clymenia

This ammonoid has a very smooth shell ornamented only with faint ribs, which radiate from the deeply set umbilicus. The sutures, when visible, are simple. The coiling is evolute, all the whorls being readily seen. An unusual feature is the dorsal siphuncle.

Size The genus grew to about 80mm (3.2in) in diameter.
Distribution *Clymenia* is found in strata of Devonian age in Europe. The specimen illustrated is from Poland.

Goniatites

This genus has involute coiling. The unsectioned specimen shows this feature, with all the inner whorls being obscured by the bulbous outer whorl. The suture lines have some complexity, with alternating rounded and pointed sections. There is no detailed ornamentation on the shell. The sectioned specimen illustrated clearly shows the internal division of the shell into buoyancy chambers. This specimen is incomplete because no large body chamber is present.
Size An ammonoid that grew to about 50mm (2in) in diameter.

Distribution *Goniatites* is found in strata of Carboniferous age in North America, Europe, north Africa and Asia. The specimen illustrated is from northern England.

Sudeticeras

This goniatite has a small, involute shell with only the outermost whorl showing, the inner whorls being totally obscured. The shell has an overall globular shape. There is no distinct ornamentation; very fine, slightly curved lines radiate from the umbilicus, and are most clearly visible in that region of the shell.

Size *Sudeticeras* grew to about 40mm (1.6in) in diameter.
Distribution A genus from the Carboniferous strata of North America, Europe, north Africa and Eurasia.

Gastrioceras

This genus is characterized by a series of prominent nodes around the umbilical margin, which develop into faint ribs across the ventral surface of the shell. The coiling is involute, the outer, rather bulbous whorl covering most of the inner whorls. The shell has an overall massive and thickset appearance.

Size This goniatite grew to about 100mm (4in) in diameter.
Distribution *Gastrioceras* is found in rocks of Carboniferous age in North America, Europe, north Africa and Asia. The specimen illustrated is from Lancashire, UK.

Prolecanites

This specimen has none of the outer shell remaining and the characteristic suture lines are very apparent. These have rounded curves pointing toward the aperture of the shell and sharp curves that face the opposite direction. The whorls of this genus are flattened and have more evolute coiling than *Gastrioceras*, with most of the inner whorls being visible. That this shell is incomplete can be told from the septal sutures reaching right to the end of the outermost whorl, proving that none of the body chamber is present.

Size This genus grew to 200mm (8in) in diameter. **Distribution** It is from Carboniferous rocks in North America, Europe and Asia.

Cladiscites

With a very involute shell, the inner whorls of *Cladiscites* are totally obscured by the large, rounded outer whorl, which widens across the ventral surface. The shell in this specimen is quite worn down, and the complex suture lines are clearly visible.

Size A medium-sized ammonoid growing to about 200mm (8in) in diameter. **Distribution** This genus is found in rocks of Triassic age in Europe (excluding the UK), Alaska and the Himalayas. The specimen shown is from Austria.

Joannites

A genus with a rounded, almost globular shell, which is coiled in such an involute manner that the presence of inner whorls could only be detected by cutting the specimen. There is little ornamentation on the shell surface other than very faint ribs. The umbilicus is a small, circular hollow in the centre of the shell.

Size The specimen shown is typical, at 60mm (2.4in) in diameter.
Distribution This genus is found in rocks of Triassic age in North America, the Himalayas and Europe (excluding the UK).

Monophyllites

This genus is one of the first members of the phylloceratid group to develop in the early Triassic. The group was abundant and important in the Jurassic. It has a thin shell with involute coiling, some of the inner whorls being visible. The shell is ornamented with thin, closely packed ribs, which curve forward over the ventral surface.

Size A typical size for this genus is about 100mm (4in) in diameter.
Distribution *Monophyllites* is found in rocks of Triassic age in North America, Europe (excluding the UK) and Asia.

Hildoceras

Hildoceras bifrons, a species of this well-known genus of ammonite, is a zone index fossil for part of the Upper Lias (Lower Jurassic). It has a sub-evolute shell structure, most of the inner whorls showing. The ribs are characteristically sickle-shaped, and there is a keel along the ventral margin of the shell, with a furrow on either side of it. Suture lines are visible on the specimen.

Size This genus grew to about 120mm (4.8in) in diameter.

Distribution It is found in rocks of Lower Jurassic age in Europe, Asia Minor and Japan. The specimen illustrated is from North Yorkshire, UK.

Echioceras

This ammonite has an openly coiled, evolute shell. The main ornamentation is in the form of thick, well-spaced ribs, which radiate from the umbilicus. A thin keel runs round the ventral surface, cutting the ribs. A species of this genus, *Echioceras raricostatum*, is a zone index fossil for part of the Lower Lias (Lower Jurassic).

Size *Echioceras* grew to about 100mm (4in) in diameter.

Distribution This genus is found in rocks of Lower Jurassic age worldwide. The specimen illustrated is from Dorset, UK.

Promicroceras

This genus of ammonite has evolute coiling of the whorls, which are almost circular in cross-section. The main shell ornamentation is a series of widely spaced, thick ribs which become flat as they cross the ventral surface. The amazing specimen of rock, crowded with the shells of this small ammonite, shows some with shell intact and others that have lost part of their shell to reveal the suture lines.

Size *Promicroceras* grew to a maximum diameter of about 30mm (1.2in).

Distribution It is found in rocks of Jurassic age in Europe.

Dactylioceras

An ammonite genus with serpenticone (snake-like) coiling,
Dactylioceras has evolute whorls that are almost round in cross-
section, apart from the slight saddle where they rest on the
next innermost whorl. The many ribs bifurcate (split in two) as
they cross the venter. In some species small tubercles are
arranged in rows on the inner whorls. The specimen shown is
preserved in a pyritized concretion, allowing an excellent
three-dimensional fossil to be formed.
Size This genus grew to 100mm (4in) in diameter.

Distribution It is
found in Lower
Jurassic strata
worldwide. The
specimen
illustrated is from
North Yorkshire,
UK.

Arnioceras

A genus of ammonite with evolute coiling. The shell is
ornamented with quite stout, well-spaced ribs, which curve
forward as they meet the ventral surface. Along this surface
there is a keel with a narrow groove on either side. This
specimen is of considerable interest because of the
preservation of the anaptychus near the aperture of the shell.
This acted as part of the jaw mechanism of the creature.
Size The genus grew to about 50mm (2in) in diameter.

Distribution It is
found in strata of
Lower Jurassic age
worldwide. The species
Arnioceras semicostatum
is a zone ammonite for
part of the Lower Lias.

Harpoceras

This ammonite shell is coiled with involute whorls, which overlap a great deal. Only part of the inner whorls can be seen. The shell is relatively flat and very narrow in cross-section. There is a keel running round the ventral surface. The ribs ornamenting the shell are typically sickle-shaped, a good indication of this genus.

Size *Harpoceras* grew to about 200mm (8in) in diameter.
Distribution The genus is found in strata of Lower Jurassic age worldwide. The species *Harpoceras falciferum* is a zone ammonite for part of the Upper Lias.

Pleuroceras

This ammonite has sub-evolute coiling of its whorls. In cross-section these whorls are rectangular. The shell is ornamented with very stout, well-spaced ribs, which may have tubercles on them and are sometimes spinose. There is a wavy keel running around the ventral surface. The specimen illustrated has much of its shell missing, and the complex ammonitic suture lines are visible.
Size The genus grew to about 100mm (4in) in diameter.

Distribution It is found in rocks of Lower Jurassic age in Europe and north Africa. The specimen illustrated is from Germany. *Pleuroceras spinatum* is a zone index fossil for part of the Middle Lias.

Lytoceras

This ammonite shell has evolute coiling, and the whorls have a rounded cross-section, becoming rapidly larger towards the aperture. The shell is ornamented with many fine, radiating ribs, which wave slightly at the margins of the whorls. There can be stronger ribs near the aperture of complete specimens. The specimen illustrated shows a broken shell with only part of the outer whorl present.

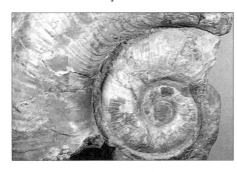

Size A genus of medium-sized ammonites, on average reaching about 150mm (6in) in diameter. **Distribution** *Lytoceras* is found in rocks of Jurassic age worldwide.

Psiloceras

This is an important genus because the species *Psiloceras planorbis* is the zone fossil for the oldest zone of the Jurassic period. Usually it is crushed flat on shale bedding planes, but this fine specimen shows a number of shells preserved in three dimensions. The shell has sub-evolute coiling, and the whorls have little ornamentation, apart from indistinct ribs. Suture lines can be seen on the shells illustrated, and as these stop before the aperture is reached, at least part of the body chamber must be present.

Size The genus grew to about 70mm (2.8in) in diameter.

Distribution It is found in Lower Jurassic rocks in North America, South America, Europe, north Africa and Indonesia.

Amaltheus

This genus has a very flattened shell with involute coiling. The shell is ornamented with radiating ribs, which curve forward as they cross the ventral surface. The keel, which follows the venter, is corded. In the specimen shown the inner whorls are obscured by sediment. This ammonite occurs in a variety of sedimentary rocks, including limestones and sandstones.

Size *Amaltheus* grew to about 80mm (3.2in) in diameter.
Distribution The genus is found in rocks of Lower Jurassic age in North America, Europe, north Africa and Asia. The species *Amaltheus margaritatus* is a zone fossil for part of the Middle Lias.

Tragophylloceras

This ammonite has an involute shell, with the inner whorls almost totally obscured by the outermost whorl. The shape is not unlike that of *Nautilus*. The shell ornamentation consists of numerous closely spaced ribs. One of the two specimens shown has the shell partly broken, revealing the sutures.
Size *Tragophylloceras* grew to about 90mm (3.6in) in diameter.
Distribution The genus is found in rocks of Lower Jurassic age worldwide. The species *Tragophylloceras ibex* is a zone index fossil for part of the Lower Lias.

Asteroceras

This ammonite shell has sub-evolute coiling, with most of the inner whorls showing. The shell is ornamented with widely spaced, thick ribs, and there is a keel with a groove on either side on the ventral surface. The ribs curve forward as they reach the venter. The buoyancy chambers of this specimen are infilled with pale calcite, and the body chamber is full of sediment.

Size The genus grows to about 100mm (4in) in diameter.
Distribution It is found in Lower Jurassic strata in North America, Europe and Asia. *Asteroceras obtusum* is a zone ammonite for part of the Lower Lias.

Morrisiceras

This genus of ammonite has a very rounded shell outline and a deep umbilicus. The outer whorl overlaps the inner whorls, giving an involute shell. Ornamentation consists of thin ribs which cross the venter but are absent on the sides of the whorl. The ribs on the inner whorls bifurcate, whereas those on the outer whorl do not.

Size The shell grew to about 80mm (3.2in) in diameter.
Distribution A genus from the Middle Jurassic strata of Europe.

Stephanoceras

This ammonite has a shell with evolute coiling, the inner whorls being clearly visible. It is ornamented with strong ribs which bifurcate and trifurcate (split into two and three) as they cross the ventral surface. There may be prominent tubercles on the umbilical margin. The whorls are rounded in cross-section.

Size The shell may be up to 150mm (6in) in diameter.
Distribution It is found in rocks of Middle Jurassic age worldwide. The specimen illustrated is from Dorset, UK. *Stephanoceras humphriesianum* is a zone fossil for part of the Middle Jurassic.

Kosmoceras

A genus with involute coiling, which is ornamented with ribs bearing spines and nodes. The ventral surface is flat.
This specimen is typically preserved crushed flat on a clay bedding plane. *Kosmoceras* is a genus which exhibits sexual dimorphism. The fossil shown is the microconch (m), distinguished by its smaller shell and lappet. This is the strange extension of the shell from the aperture. The macroconch (M) lacks a lappet. This genus has been studied extensively, and provides a classic evolutionary sequence.

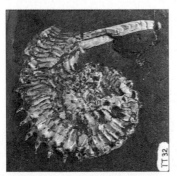

Size This form of the genus reached 60mm (2.4in) in diameter.
Distribution It is found in rocks of Middle Jurassic age worldwide. *Kosmoceras jason* is a zone index species.

Brasilia (M) & *Ludwigella* (m)

A dimorphic pair of ammonites exhibiting a great size difference. These two, preserved in the same bed of oolitic limestone, have very similar features. Both ammonites are involute in their coiling, with the outer whorl obscuring most of the inner whorls. The shell ornamentation consists of numerous sickle-shaped ribs, which curve forward just before crossing the ventral surface. There is a sharp, well-developed keel. When complete, the microconch (m) has a lappet at the aperture of the shell, whereas the macroconch (M) has a simple aperture.

Size *Brasilia* grew to about 200mm (8in) in diameter; the relative size of *Ludwigella* can be judged from the specimens shown.

Distribution These ammonites are found in Middle Jurassic strata in Europe, Iran and north Africa. The specimen illustrated is from Dorset, UK.

Liparoceras (M) & *Aegoceras* (m)

These two ammonites are shown together because they are believed to be a dimorphic pair. One is the male and the other the female. The rules of naming fossils say that the first name officially given is the one used, so this pair retains its differing generic names. *Liparoceras*, the macroconch (M), is a stout shell with thick, well-spaced ribs which bifurcate as they cross the broad ventral surface. It has involute coiling, only a small part of the inner whorls being visible. The ribs have pairs of sharp spines on them near the venter and above the umbilicus. *Aegoceras*, the microconch (m), is evolute in its coiling, and strong ribs cross the shell. Weak tubercles can occur on the ribs. Sexual dimorphism in ammonites is recognized by many factors. This pair, for example, have a similar stratigraphic range and developed the same characteristics.

Size *Liparoceras* grew to about 100mm (4in) in diameter. *Aegoceras* reached only about 60mm (2.4in).

Distribution They both occur in Lower Jurassic rocks. The macroconch has been recorded in Europe, north Africa and Indonesia. The microconch has been found in Europe. The specimens illustrated are from Gloucestershire, UK.

Procerites (M) & *Siemiradzkia* (m)

These two ammonites are a sexually dimorphic pair and have a tremendous size difference. The two shells are mature and complete. On close examination of the specimens the suture lines are found to finish well before the shell aperture, indicating that a greater proportion of the final and largest whorl of the shell is occupied by the body chamber, which is not divided by septa. *Procerites* (M) is a sub-evolute shell with broad, flattened whorls. There is little shell ornamentation in this specimen, though when less worn there are numerous radiating ribs which bifurcate as they cross the venter. *Siemiradzkia* (m) is very much smaller and has sub-evolute shell coiling. The whorls are ornamented with many ribs, which split as they cross the venter.

Size *Procerites* is a very large ammonite, growing to well over 300mm (12in) in diameter. *Siemiradzkia* grew to only about 40mm (1.6in) in diameter.

Distribution Both ammonites are from the Middle Jurassic worldwide. The specimens illustrated are from Cape Mondego, Spain.

Ludwigia (M) & Ludwigina (m)

Another dimorphic pair of ammonites with widely differing shell sizes. *Ludwigia* has involute coiling of its whorls, but the umbilicus is clearly visible. There is a steep umbilical margin and the shell is ornamented with ribs, which have a characteristic sickle shape. These ribs bifurcate well before they reach the ventral surface. There is a sharp, narrow keel on the venter. *Ludwigina* is very like the inner whorls of *Ludwigia*, with similar coiling of the whorls and ornamentation. The suture lines on the specimen end just after the start of the outer whorl. This indicates that the specimen is complete because the part of the shell divided into chambers by septa corresponds with the occurrence of suture lines, each suture line marking the position of a septum. The majority of the outer whorl is therefore the undivided body chamber.

Size *Ludwigia* grew to about 120mm (4.8in) in diameter, *Ludwigina* being far smaller. The relative proportions can be seen in the illustration.

Distribution These ammonites are found in Middle Jurassic strata in Europe, north Africa, Iran, Siberia and South America. *Ludwigia murchisonae* is a zone fossil for part of the Middle Jurassic.

Chondroceras

This ammonite has a bulbous shell with involute coiling of the whorls, which have a rounded cross-section. The main ornamentation consists of many ribs which bifurcate and trifurcate along the margin of the outer whorl before they cross the venter.

Size A small ammonite, reaching about 40mm (1.6in) in diameter.
Distribution It is found in rocks of Middle Jurassic age in North America, South America, Europe, north Africa, Papua New Guinea and Indonesia.

Sphaeroceras

An ammonite with a bulbous shell and involute coiling, the umbilicus being closed. The aperture has a flared collar and the shell is ornamented with curved ribs, which bifurcate across the ventral surface. The whorls have an oval cross-section, the last whorl being incompletely coiled.

Size A genus of small ammonites, reaching only about 30mm (1.2in) in diameter.
Distribution It is found in rocks of Middle Jurassic age in Alaska, Iran, north Africa and Europe. The specimen illustrated is from Bayeux, France.

Witchellia

The coiling of this ammonite shell is involute, the umbilicus hardly being visible. The shell is ornamented with ribs, and there is a prominent keel around the venter. Most of the outer shell is missing from the specimen shown, and the suture lines are clearly visible, especially near the location label. The microconch of this genus developed a rostrum, and the lappet

curved inwards, constricting the aperture.

Size This genus grew to about 100mm (4in) in diameter.

Distribution It is found in Middle Jurassic rocks in Europe.

Parkinsonia

A common ammonite, *Parkinsonia* has an evolute shell, with all the whorls clearly visible. This type of coiling is referred to as serpenticone. The shell ornamentation consists of radiating ribs which bifurcate as they cross the venter. These ribs are interrupted by a smooth band running around the ventral surface. The whorls have a compressed cross-section.

Size This genus grew to about 150mm (6in) in diameter.

Distribution It is found in rocks of Middle Jurassic age in Europe, Asia, north Africa and Iran. *Parkinsonia parkinsoni* is a zone fossil for part of the Middle Jurassic.

Graphoceras

With involute coiling, this ammonite shell has a large outer whorl. The weak ribs are sickle-shaped and split into two parts where they cross the venter. The cross-section of the whorls is very flat. The venter is sharp and the umbilical shoulder is steep. The very pale specimen illustrated is preserved in oolitic limestone.

Size *Graphoceras* grew to about 80mm (3.2in) in diameter.
Distribution A genus found in Middle Jurassic strata in Europe, Asia and Africa. *Graphoceras concavum* is a zone index species for part of the Middle Jurassic.

Cardioceras

This shell has involute coiling, only a small part of the inner whorls being visible. There are strong ribs crossing the shell; these bifurcate before they cross the venter. There may be tubercles at the point of bifurcation. The microconchs of this genus have an extension of the aperture. The macroconchs lack ornamentation on their body chambers, and

are about twice the size of the microconchs.
Size The genus grew to about 60mm (2.4in) in diameter.
Distribution It is found in rocks of Upper Jurassic age worldwide. *Cardioceras cordatum* is a zone ammonite.

Quenstedtoceras

Two examples are illustrated, one being a broken specimen which shows the internal buoyancy chambers. This ammonite has a sub-evolute shell ornamented with strong ribs, which bifurcate along the side of the outer whorl. The microconch is shown, the macroconch having far less shell ornamentation. Complete shells have an extension on the aperture called a rostrum.

Size This genus, in microconch form as shown, grew to about

60mm (2.4in) in diameter.
Distribution It is found in Middle and Upper Jurassic strata worldwide. Two species, *Quenstedtoceras lamberti* and *Q. mariae*, are zone fossils.

Pavlovia

This specimen is virtually crushed on a shale bedding plane but some of the original calcareous material of the shell is present as a white film. The shell has sub-evolute coiling and is crossed by widely spaced ribs, which bifurcate across the venter. The whorls are circular in cross-section.

Size The genus grew to about 200mm (8in) in diameter.

Distribution It is found in Upper Jurassic strata in Greenland, Asia, and Europe. Two species, *Pavlovia rotunda* and *P. pallasioides*, are zone fossils.

Amoeboceras

This ammonite shell is of interest because it shows a feature recognized as indicating maturity of the individual creature. The suture lines, clearly visible on the shell, crowd together towards the aperture. These end where the body chamber begins, showing that the specimen is virtually complete. This ammonite has involute coiling and fine ribs as ornamentation. A corded keel runs round the venter of some species.

Size A genus which grew to about 80mm (3.2in) in diameter.
Distribution It is from Upper Jurassic rocks in Europe.

Titanites

This genus has evolute coiling and is ornamented with well-spaced, strong ribs. These bifurcate as they cross the ventral surface. The ribs become crowded together on the outer whorl. The specimen shown has characteristic dark colouring near the aperture.

Size *Titanites* is one of the largest of the ammonites, growing to well over 1 metre (39in) in diameter. Such specimens are difficult to collect.

Distribution It is found in rocks of Upper Jurassic age in northern Europe, Greenland, Canada and Asia. The specimen illustrated is from Dorset, UK, and is on display in the Department of Geology, University of Keele, Staffordshire, UK. *Titanites giganteus* is a zone fossil.

Sigaloceras

This ammonite shell is preserved in pyrite and has small nodules of the mineral adhering to the fossil. It has involute coiling, and the whorls are ornamented with fine ribs, some of which are more pronounced than others. In some species the venter is flattened. The suture lines are clearly visible on the specimen shown. This genus exhibits sexual dimorphism. The microconchs develop a lappet.

Size The genus grew to about 60mm (2.4in) in diameter.
Distribution It is found in rocks of Upper Jurassic age in Europe. *Sigaloceras calloviense* is a zone fossil.

Turrilites

This genus of ammonites is different from the majority in that the shell is helicoid (coiled in a spiral), reminiscent of a gastropod shell. However, being an ammonite, it has typical suture lines visible when some of the outer shell is removed. This shell is ornamented with weak ribs and well-formed tubercles. This ammonite probably swam with its buoyant shell extended upwards.

Size *Turrilites* reached about 150mm (6in) in length.
Distribution The genus is found in strata of Cretaceous age worldwide. The specimen illustrated is from southern England.

Mantelliceras

This ammonite shell has involute coiling, with only part of the inner whorls visible. It is ornamented with thick ribs, which have two rows of tubercles where they cross the ventral surface. Small tubercles may be present at the umbilical margin.
Size *Mantelliceras* grew to about 100mm (4in) in diameter.

Distribution This genus is found in Cretaceous strata in the USA, Europe, north Africa, India and south-east Asia. The specimen illustrated is from northern France. It occurs with other ammonites and bivalve molluscs.

Endemoceras

This ammonite shell has involute coiling, only part of the inner whorls being visible. These become rapidly larger; each whorl being much larger than its predecessor. The shell ornamentation consists of stout ribs which split in two before they cross the ventral surface. The specimen is from the Lower Cretaceous Speeton clay deposit of east Yorkshire, where it occurs with other fossils, including ammonites and belemnites.

Size The specimen is typical, at about 40mm (1.6in) in diameter.
Distribution *Endemoceras* is found in rocks of Lower Cretaceous age in Europe.

Euhoplites

This shell has coiling which is sub-evolute. The umbilicus is deeply set and the inner whorls are partly visible. The ventral surface of the shell has a deep groove along it and the shell is ornamented with stout ribs which may have nodes near the

venter. The ribs curve as they cross the venter.
Size *Euhoplites* has a diameter of about 50mm (2.0in).
Distribution It is found in rocks of Lower Cretaceous age in Greenland, Alaska and northern Europe. The specimen illustrated is from Kent, UK. *Euhoplites latus* is a zone fossil.

Baculites

This uncoiled ammonite is in general shape reminiscent of the large, uncoiled nautiloids of the lower Palaeozoic. The early stages are minute and coiled. Unfortunately, this ammonite is commonly found as incomplete broken fragments, as illustrated. It is easily told from orthocone nautiloids by the complex, typically ammonitic suture lines, which are very well displayed in this specimen. The ventral surface can be ornamented with ribs and tubercles, and there is an extension called a rostrum on one side of the shell aperture.

Size This genus grew to 2 metres (78in) in length.

Distribution It is found in rocks of Upper Cretaceous age worldwide. The specimen illustrated is from South Dakota, USA.

Acanthoscaphites

This ammonite has a somewhat strange shell, with slight uncoiling of the outermost whorl. The shell is involute, the large outer whorl covering the tightly coiled inner whorls. The shell is flattened and broad. Ornamentation consists of numerous closely spaced ribs, which curve slightly near the umbilicus. There are also tubercles on the ventral and umbilical margins. The aperture has a hooked appearance, and faces the rest of the shell. This ammonite shows strong sexual dimorphism.

Size The genus has a diameter of about 50mm (2.0in).

Distribution It is found in rocks of Cretaceous age in North America, South Africa, Chile, Australia and Europe. The specimen shown is from South Dakota, USA.

Hamites

This is another bizarre ammonite, often found as straight, broken sections of shell, as illustrated. The whole shell has up to three uncoiled parts joined by sharp curves, and has an oval or circular cross-section. It is ornamented with encircling ribs.

Size The genus grew to about 65mm (2.6in) in length.

Distribution *Hamites* is found in rocks of Lower Cretaceous age in North America, Europe and Asia.

Anahoplites

This ammonite has a very flattened, compressed shell and whorls which are sub-evolute in their coiling. The umbilicus is clearly visible and the umbilical margin is steep. There are weak ribs ornamenting the shell and slight nodes may be present on the umbilical margin.

Size *Anahoplites* grew to about 100mm (4in) in diameter.
Distribution The genus is found in rocks of Lower Cretaceous age in Europe and Asia.

Laevaptychus

This fossil is associated with the ammonoids and is sometimes found inside the body chamber of an ammonite shell, or appearing to close the shell aperture. Its purpose has been open to debate; it was regarded as an operculum which acted as a door on the aperture of the shell, but now it is thought to be part of the jaw mechanism. The structure has a sub-triangular shape. One side is concave with concentric lines around it, while the other surface is convex and pitted.
Size The specimens illustrated are about 60mm (2.4in) across. Such fossils vary with the ammonite species to which they are related.

Distribution They are found in Jurassic strata worldwide.

Coleoidea (Order Belemnitida)

The coleoids are the squids, octopods and cuttles, well known in the modern oceans. They are closely related to the extinct ammonites; indeed, the squids and cuttles are more closely related to the ammonites than ammonites are to the similar-looking *Nautilus*.

The belemnites (Belemnitida) are familiar fossils, especially in marine strata of Mesozoic age. They can be found in rocks ranging from Lower Carboniferous to Tertiary, and are strange, bullet- or cigar-shaped fossils of thick calcareous construction, often with a sharply pointed end. If more or less complete, a larger structure with concentric chambered divisions, the phragmacone, can be found, either joined to the wider end of the shell or as a separate fossil. Most belemnites are quite small, but they can reach about 200mm (8in) in length. They are very difficult fossils to collect, as they easily break when an attempt is made to remove them from rock. The belemnite fossil is the internal guard of a squid-like creature, which had tentacles, eyes and an ink sac.

Acrocoelites

Here a shale bedding plane is covered with the shells of this belemnite genus. Fossils and other objects that are long and thin are often aligned as these belemnites are, with their long axes parallel. The obvious inference is that they were orientated by a water current flowing near the sea-bed. Most of the shells on the specimen illustrated are of the broken guards, but in one or two the end of the phragmacone can be seen inside the blunt end of the fossil, especially where the shell has been split in half by weathering and erosion of the rock strata.

Size A genus up to 120mm (4.8in) in length.
Distribution It is from Lower Jurassic rocks in Europe and North America.

Actinocamax

This genus has a lanceolate guard. The cross-section is sub-quadrate and there are lines on the surface. A groove runs along the ventral part of the fossil. The shell surface is often granular and may have impressions left by the vascular tissue.
Size This belemnite is never of great size, and the specimen shown is typical at 75mm (3.0in) in length.

Distribution
Actinocamax is found in Upper Cretaceous sediments in Greenland, Europe and Asia.

Belemnitella

This common genus has a cylindrical guard ornamented with grooves and lines. These spread apart near the apex, which has a small, pointed tip. Vascular impressions are not uncommon.
Size The specimens shown are about 100mm (4in) in length.

Distribution
Belemnitella is found in Upper Cretaceous rocks in North America, Europe, Asia and Greenland.

Animals - Vertebrates

This group of fossils includes the remains of fish, amphibians, reptiles, birds and mammals. These creatures are not as common in the fossil record as the invertebrates for a number of reasons. Many invertebrates live in the sea, so when they die they can be rapidly covered with sediment and preserved. This is true of only some of the vertebrate groups. Many of them live on land, where sedimentation tends to be replaced by processes of weathering and erosion, so their remains are fragmented rather than buried. However, there are areas in North America, China and Africa where great numbers of reptile and other vertebrate skeletons are preserved, often in rocks laid down in rivers and lakes. It is rare to come across a complete skeleton; in fact, to find a few teeth or a single vertebra is often all that can be expected.

Another reason for the predominance of invertebrate fossils is that the vertebrates developed much later in time. Primitive reptiles, the Thecodonts, evolved during the Carboniferous, and it was only during the Jurassic and Cretaceous periods that the reptiles became dominant. The early mammals are found in strata of Triassic age, but it was not until the Tertiary era that they developed fully.

Bone bed

Vertebrate fossils are often fragmented and accumulate in masses, as in this specimen of the Triassic bone bed of southern England. It contains numerous bone fragments and teeth set in a rock matrix. Teeth are very durable parts of creatures, and are sometimes the only evidence we have of their former existence. The best preserved tooth on this slab is of the fish *Hybodus*.

Fish

Fish are probably the commonest vertebrates in the fossil record. An important reason for this is that they live in water, where much deposition of sediment takes place, so they can be rapidly buried and preserved. Many of these creatures have strong, bony skeletons and also a covering of resistant scales. Both these features help their fossilization, but fish teeth are also an important part of the fossil record.

The first fish, which were probably the first vertebrates, lived during the Ordovician period and developed during the Silurian and Devonian periods. These Agnathans (jawless fish) have only the primitive lampreys and hagfish as descendants. Many of the early fish lived in brackish and fresh water, and are known from continental lake and river deposits, especially of Devonian age. It was during this period that the Osteichthyes, the true bony fish, appeared. The Jurassic period saw the development of the Teleosts, the group to which most modern fish belong. A most important group, the Dinopans, or lung-fish, are found in rocks of Devonian to Recent age. They are able to survive out of water and they have many similarities to the early amphibians.

Holoptychius

This herring-sized fish is characterized by lobed fins which have dermal bones. The tail is heterocercal, having the vertebra in the upper lobe, which is larger than the lower one. The body is covered with large, rounded scales. Great numbers of these fish have been found fossilized together, suggesting a sudden drying out of the environment in which they lived.

Size *Holoptychius* grew to about 500mm (20in) in length.

Distribution It is found in non-marine strata of Upper Devonian to Lower Carboniferous age. The specimen shown is from Fife, Scotland.

Glyptolepis

This fine specimen is preserved in an iron-rich concretion. The large scales covering the body are well displayed. These are thin and rounded, and may have small ridges or tubercles. This bony fish has an elongated body with the fins set well back near the tail; only the front half of the fish is seen here. The fins are paired, and the tail has a larger upper lobe.
Size The fossil illustrated would be 150mm (6in) long if complete.

Distribution A freshwater fish from rocks of Devonian age. The specimen shown is from Nairn, Scotland.

Gyroptychius

This specimen shows almost complete preservation. The body is covered with small, diamond-shaped scales. The stumpy tail is placed centrally around the spinal vertebra, and the paired fins are well to the back of the body. The head is armoured with larger plates.
Size The genus grew to about 70mm (2.8in) in length.
Distribution *Gyroptychius* occurs in non-marine strata of Devonian age. The specimen illustrated is from Orkney, Scotland.

Ischnacanthus

The genus is characterized by a slender body with a longer upper lobe in its tail. There are two dorsal and three ventral spines. This fish lived in freshwater conditions and was one of the first true jawed fish. The mouth is filled with many small teeth.

Size *Ischnacanthus* grew to about 60mm (2.4in) in length.
Distribution It is found in non-marine rocks of Devonian age. The specimen illustrated is from Kinnaird, Scotland.

Osteolepis

This fish has a tapering body with two dorsal fins and three ventral fins. The tail has a larger upper lobe. The scales are diamond-shaped and the head is covered with larger plates. The mouth contains numerous small teeth, possibly indicating a carnivorous diet.

Size *Osteolepis* grew to about 120mm (4.8in) in length.
Distribution This genus is of Devonian age and occurs in freshwater sediments in Europe and Asia. The specimen illustrated is from Banff, Scotland.

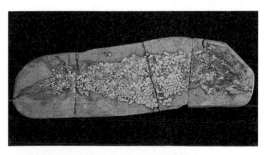

Cheirolepis

This specimen is virtually complete and shows a slender freshwater fish with small, square scales covering the body. There is a large, solitary dorsal fin, and the upper lobe of the tail is larger than the lower one.

Size This genus grew to about 350mm (14in) in length.

Distribution It is found in Middle and Upper Devonian rocks. The specimen shown is from Clune, Scotland.

Cephalaspis

This genus of fossil fish is characterized by a very large head-shield, which curves backward with pointed extensions. There are small eyeholes in the middle of the upper surface. The small mouth, which is underneath, was probably adapted to suction feeding. There are gill slits behind the mouth. The slender body is eel-like and the fish probably moved with a wriggling motion. The brain is thought to have been similar to that of the modern lamprey.

Size This small fish grew to about 100mm (4in) in length.

Distribution It is found in rocks ranging in age from Upper Silurian to Middle Devonian, deposited in fresh water. The specimen illustrated is from Angus, Scotland.

Bothriolepis

This photograph shows the body and head shield of a genus that is characterized by having two bony appendages extending from the head shield. The body, apart from the fragment shown here, has no scales, and is thin and eel-like. It belongs to the group called Placoderms and has paired fins and simple jaws. The tail has a large upper lobe and a smaller lower one.

Size The specimen shown is about 90mm (3.6in) long.

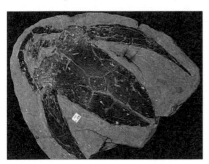

Distribution
Bothriolepis occurs in freshwater rocks of Devonian age worldwide. The specimen is from Scaumenac Bay, Canada.

Dipterus

This genus of lung-fish has characteristic jaws, with flattened teeth in the palate and the floor of the mouth for crushing small invertebrates. Some modern lung fish can survive out of water in burrows in the mud, while others gulp air from the water surface. *Dipterus* has bony strengthening in its fins and a thickset body.

Size A small fish growing to about 70mm (2.8in) in length.

Distribution It is found in Middle Devonian strata. The specimen illustrated is from the Achnaharras fishbeds of Scotland.

Platysomus

This modern-looking fish has been beautifully preserved in fine-grained limestone. It has a very deep body and a tail with lobes of equal length. The fins are almost triangular in shape and unpaired. The scales, clearly seen in the specimen illustrated, are lengthened dorsoventrally (from top to bottom). *Platysomus* belongs to the Actinopterygian group of fish, being ray-finned and breathing with gills. This genus has conical teeth. This fish and many others are fossilized in the Marl Slate deposit of north-east England. This formation is of Lower Permian age. The term slate should strictly be reserved for rocks of metamorphic origin, the name Marl Slate being an anglicized form of the German word 'Mergelschiefer'. The Marl Slate is a shale containing much silt and dolomite, commonly with very fine bedding laminations. It formed when the Zechstein Sea covered north-east England, and may have taken only about 20,000 years to be deposited. It has been estimated that this sea, in which *Platysomus* lived, was around 150 metres (500 feet) deep. Eventually this sea retreated eastwards, and a thick evaporite sequence was formed.

Size The specimen illustrated is about 70mm (2.8in) long.

Distribution *Platysomus* ranges in age from Lower Carboniferous to Upper Permian. The specimen shown is from Durham, UK.

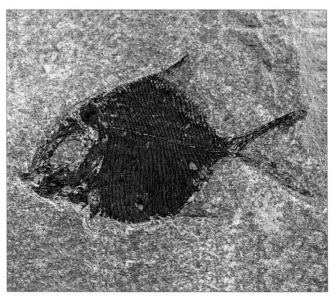

Acrolepis

A fish often of large size, *Acrolepis* is seen here well preserved in fine-grained sediment, with only part of the head and tail missing. The body is covered with coarse, diamond-shaped scales, clearly seen towards the tail on this specimen. The head is usually about a quarter of the whole length. Both pectoral and pelvic fins are present.

Size This genus grew to 400mm (16in) in length.

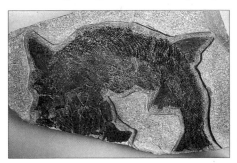

Distribution It occurs in marine rocks ranging in age from Carboniferous to Permian in Britain, Germany, Africa, Greenland and the CIS. The specimen is from Permian strata in Durham, UK.

Dapedius

This fish belongs to the group called the Holosteans, which are covered with bony plates rather than scales, and were superseded by the Teleosts during the Jurassic period. *Dapedius* has a typical rounded outline, and the large rectangular plates covering the body are clearly seen in the specimen illustrated. The head is protected by larger plates and the small mouth contains thin, sharp teeth. There is a long dorsal fin, a short tail, which has an upper supporting structure, and a long anal fin.

Size It usually grew to about 200mm (8in) in length.
Distribution A genus from marine rocks of Lower Jurassic age. The specimen shown is from southern England.

Leptolepis

This fish belongs to the Osteichthyes group of bony fish and
has many of the characteristics of modern fish. It has a small but
elongate, tapering body, and a small mouth with many teeth.
There is a small, central dorsal fin. The equally lobed tail is
clearly seen in this specimen.
Size *Leptolepis* grew to about 120mm (4.8in).

Distribution
A common marine
fish in rocks of
Upper Triassic to
Cretaceous age in
North America,
Europe, Asia and
South Africa.

Gosiutichthys

This slab of fine-grained sediment shows a typical preservation of
this small Teleost fish, as a shoal killed when the lake in which they
lived dried out. It is a modern type of fish and fed from the water
surface. The excellent preservation seen here gives details of the
skeleton and size variation. The Teleosts are the most numerous
fishes of today, having over 24,000 species.
Size *Gosiutichthys* grew to about 500mm (20in) in length.
Distribution This genus is of Tertiary age, and the specimen
illustrated is from the well-known Eocene deposits at Green River,
Wyoming, USA.

Amphibians *Temnospondyl*

This is a most important fossil because it is the earliest complete amphibian skeleton known. It is preserved in limestone and shows the skull, front and hind limbs, and body. The hands have four digits and the feet five. Its mode of life was by no means exclusively aquatic. The word 'temnospondyl' is not a generic name, but refers to the group of tetrapods to which the fossil is assigned. This fossil was found with a fauna of scorpions, spiders, myrapods and amphibians. This group of organisms, and the fact that there are no associated fossil fishes, indicates that the environment of deposition of the limestone containing them was terrestrial rather than in water. As well as this virtually entire skeleton, another skull, a pelvis with limbs, and various individual bones have been found.

Size The specimen is 400mm (16in) long.

Distribution It was found in rocks of Lower Carboniferous age in West Lothian, Scotland. Early tetrapods are also recorded from Upper Devonian rocks in Australia and east Greenland. The only other places where rocks of Lower Carboniferous age have yielded tetrapod fossils are one site in Nova Scotia, Canada, and two sites in West Virginia, USA.

Reptiles

Fossils of large reptiles, such as dinosaurs, are generally not very common, though in some parts of the world many have been found in small areas. Nevertheless, it is quite possible to find isolated teeth and bones, particularly those of large marine reptiles, in the same Mesozoic strata as ammonites and other molluscs.

Iguanodon

This was one of the first dinosaurs to be described and was originally known only from fossilized teeth found by Dr Gideon Mantell, a keen amateur geologist, in Sussex, UK, in 1818. It was not until 1825 that he named the creature. The specimens illustrated are a caudal vertebra *(left)* and a toe bone. *Iguanodon* was a bipedal dinosaur that walked upright, and from a study of fossils found in England, Germany and Belgium, geologists believe that it lived in herds. It had a horny, beak-like mouth and grinding teeth on the sides of the jaw. These were used for crushing plant material.

Size Adults reached a height of about 10 metres (39ft).
Distribution This dinosaur has been found fossilized in Cretaceous rocks in southern England, north Africa and Europe.

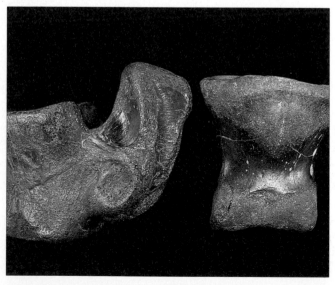

Ichthyosaurus

The specimen illustrated below shows a small part of the jaw and teeth of this streamlined marine reptile. The teeth are characteristically cone-shaped and have lengthwise grooves which increase in number towards the point. The creature was a carnivore, swimming quickly through the sea in pursuit of prey. As the reptile lived in water, it is not unusual to find fossilized teeth and fragments of its skeleton. Whole skeletons are not uncommon and have been found with a carbonaceous film showing the outline of the body, which was similar to that of the modern dolphin. Like these modern mammals, ichthyosaurs are believed to have given birth to live young; fossils of adults with young inside them have been found. The bottom photograph shows the detail of an *Ichthyosaurus* vertebra, which has been so well preserved that the original bone tissue can be clearly seen in this broken example. The bone material has been partly replaced by calcite.

Size This marine reptile grew to about 3 metres (10 feet) in length.
Distribution These fossils are found worldwide in rocks of Mesozoic age.

Plesiosaurus

This marine reptile had a rather different structure from the *Ichthyosaurus*. It had a larger, rounded body and a long, thin neck and tail. The limbs were, in effect, large flippers with a great many digit bones. These 'paddles' were the means of locomotion for this powerful creature, and recent research has shown that they were moved up and down like the wings of birds that swim underwater. Some forms had very long necks and small heads with sharp teeth in their jaws. It has been suggested that they darted their heads at moving prey, possibly fish and molluscs. Those with shorter necks may have been fierce predators and lived more like today's killer whales.

Plesiosaurus **vertebra**
A single bone, which is about 120mm (4.8in) in diameter, and a typical find. It is common for vertebrae to become disarticulated soon after the creature dies.

Plesiosaurus **limb**
This reconstruction of the hand of a *Plesiosaurus* shows the numerous small digit bones and paddle-like construction. The whole limb is about 600mm (24in) long and is from Lower Jurassic strata in North Yorkshire, UK.

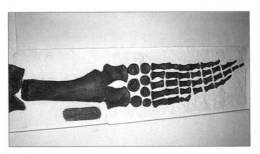

Plesiosaurus ribs

The rather bulbous body of the *Plesiosaurus* is supported by a strong ribcage, detail of which is shown in this fine specimen from Lower Jurassic strata.

Mammals *Balaena*

A rather strange-looking object, which is the ear bone of a whale. These curved bones are reasonably common in marine Tertiary strata. The structure of the smaller whales is similar to that of the marine reptiles of earlier geological times.

Size This ear bone is 55mm (2.2in) in length.

Distribution The first fossil whales appear in rocks of Eocene age. This bone is from Miocene strata.

Fossil Teeth
Merycoidodon

These are some of the teeth and part of the jaw of a plant-eating mammal sometimes called *Oreodon*. The molar teeth have four crowns and are not unlike those of cattle. *Merycoidodon* was a pig-like creature and had large upper canine teeth. Four species of this genus are recognized and classified mainly by size.

Size The fossil shown is 70mm (2.8in) long. The whole skeleton is generally the size of a small pig.

Distribution This genus is well known from the Oligocene strata of South Dakota and Nebraska, USA, and is especially numerous as fossils in the White River Beds.

Hyena

This mammal has teeth adapted for crushing bones, and the lower jaw illustrated, which comes from a cave hyena, shows such dentition. The teeth are strong and there are extended cheek teeth for slicing. Fossils of this type are not uncommon in non-marine sediments and cave deposits of late Tertiary and Recent age.

Size The specimen illustrated is 80mm (3.2in) in length.

Distribution *Hyena* is a genus from Europe, Asia and Africa found in Pliocene and Recent strata.

Mammuthus

These photographs show a cheek tooth of this large mammal. The single tooth is of great size and its surface is crossed by rough ridges and furrows. These structures are much less steep and high than in *Elephas*. Such fossils are commonly found in river gravels and other terrestrial sediments, though whole skeletons are quite rare. This genus became well adapted to living in the cold conditions on the margins of the Pleistocene ice sheet, and was of greater size than modern elephants.

Size The tooth illustrated is 250mm (10in) long.

Distribution Such fossils can be found in rocks ranging in age from Miocene to Pleistocene in North America, Europe, Asia and Africa.

This photograph shows a detail of the cheek tooth illustrated above.

Hippopotamus

This is a canine tooth from the lower jaw. *Hippopotamus* was widespread in swampy, lowland areas, especially during the interglacials of the last one million years; today it is confined to Africa. The mouth of this herbivorous ungulate contains large molar teeth, which are common as fossils.

Size This particular tooth is 100mm (4in) long.
Distribution Fossils of this type are found in rocks of Upper Pliocene age and younger in Africa, Europe and Asia.

Odontaspis

The illustration shows the teeth of an ancient shark. Representatives of the genus are alive today and reach over 4 metres (13 ft) in length. The teeth are characterized by having side cusps, which can be seen as small, sharp points very near the base of the tooth. This small selection is typical material; some are broken and some complete. Such teeth are extremely durable and therefore are preserved easily.

Size Most of the teeth illustrated are about 20mm (0.8in) long.

Distribution These fossils are found in rocks of Cretaceous to Recent age in North America, South America, Europe, Asia, Africa and New Zealand.

Rhizodus

This is a fish tooth from a genus which grew to considerable size. It has typical striations and parallel grooves towards the thicker base. The tooth tapers gradually to a blunt point. The jaw of *Rhizodus* may be over 1 metre (39in) long.
Size The specimen shown is 140mm (5.6in) long.

Distribution
Rhizodus is found in strata of Devonian and Carboniferous age worldwide. This example is from the Scottish oil shales of Carboniferous age.

Ceratodus

This lung-fish, which is closely related to *Neoceratodus* (a form living in Australia today), has teeth that are fused into flattened plates. These help the fish to crush the shelled creatures on which it feeds. The surfaces of the teeth are covered with many small dimples.
Size The fossil shown is 20mm (0.8in) long.
Distribution *Ceratodus* occurs in Mesozoic sedimentary rocks worldwide. The specimen illustrated is from the Triassic of southern England.

Charcarodon

This tooth is from a very large shark, of which only these durable objects are usually found as fossils. They are typically sub-triangular in shape and diverge into two roots at the base. The edges are serrated and designed for flesh cutting.

Size Teeth such as this are commonly 150mm (6in) long, and the shark could grow up to 15 metres (48ft) in length.
Distribution These fossils are found in rocks of Tertiary age worldwide.

Mastodon

The illustration shows part of the fossil jaw of a large, elephant-like mammal. The teeth are designed for plant eating, and have fused crowns. They show other adaptations for grazing, such as the way the crowns are high and continue to grow throughout the creature's life.
Size The jaw shown is about 180mm (7.2in) in length.
Distribution Such fossils are found in rocks of Tertiary age worldwide.

Ptychodus

Sharks can have flat teeth adapted for crushing, as well as slender, pointed teeth. This fossil tooth is typical of the former type. The ridges running across its surface are very hard and it is quite painful to press a finger against the surface, which would have been used for crushing shellfish.

Size The fossil is 45mm (1.8in) wide.
Distribution These sharks are found in Cretaceous rocks in North America, Europe, Africa and Asia.

Lamna

This is a tooth from a genus of medium-sized sharks. The surface is smooth, though some may be striated. There are typical side spikes at the lower end of the tooth. The edges, unlike those of many sharks' teeth, are not serrated.
Size This fossil is about 30mm (1.2in) long.
Distribution *Lamna* is found worldwide in rocks ranging in age from Cretaceous to Pliocene.

Trace Fossils

Fossils are not necessarily the shells, bones and other remains of organisms; they can also be the tracks, trails, burrows and dung left by creatures. These traces are of great use to palaeontologists, and are not uncommon in the fossil record. Many different creatures are responsible for producing such fossils; these include molluscs, worms, dinosaurs and arthropods. One of the uses of these fossils is to enable scientists to determine whether the rocks containing footprints or burrows have been upturned by folding. The 'way up' of the strata has to be determined before stratigraphic work is carried out. This can be done using a variety of techniques. These include the observation and investigation of certain sedimentary structures, produced by the processes which were operative when the strata were being deposited. For example, some sedimentary rocks contain a grading of their sedimentary particles, the coarser grains lying below finer material when originally formed. There are also a number of structures, like ripple marks and cross bedding, which can be used to determine 'way up' of strata. Ripple marks and dessication cracks (mud-cracks), form on a sediment surface and a footprint made on the surface of the ground or a burrow bored into the sea bed are ideal evidence for this investigation. These fossils can also be compared with modern tracks and trails, and an understanding of the lifestyle of the creatures that made them may be possible. Palaeontologists can also establish what creatures were present in a certain region, even if only their traces and not their shells or bones are preserved. The study of fossil footprints is called ichnology, and much can be learned from this work. The size and weight of the creature, its stance and speed can all be estimated.

The actual trace fossil is commonly preserved as a cast or a mould. A fossil burrow, for example, is a mould, and the sediment or minerals which fill it and preserve it form a cast. Many creatures burrow and leave trace fossils of this type, including the bivalve mollusc *Mya* and the brachiopod *Lingula*. Worm burrows, like those common in the Cambrian quartzites of northern Scotland, are well-known trace fossils, as are the trail-like burrows left by the sea-floor feeding activities of shrimps and molluscs.

As with other fossils, trace fossils are given names according to the strict system of biological nomenclature. It can happen that a burrow or trail will have a different name from that of the creature that made it. For instance, the sediment surface burrows called *Thalassinoides* are often associated with the crustacean *Glyphea*. Both are not uncommon in Jurassic sub-tidal sediments.

Satapliasaurus

This fossil footprint is of a bipedal dinosaur which roamed the muddy marshlands of the Jurassic period. The preservation of it is as a positive cast, which was found when bedding planes were split, the mould into which it fitted being on the lower bedding plane. It is not always possible to identify the creature which made a footprint, or tracks. It is possible, however, to determine its size, and whether it walked on two legs or all four. If there are many footprints on the bedding plane, the number of individuals can be determined; some dinosaurs congregated in herds. There are many examples of this fossil being found as many footprints on a single bedding plane. These can sometimes be attributed to a number of individuals, especially when the prints are of varying sizes. Recent research shows that the speeds at which creatures moved can be worked out with a certain accuracy from their footprints.

Size The example is 150mm (6in) long, although they can be as long as 600mm (24in) long.

Distribution The footprint was found in the Middle Jurassic strata of Yorkshire, UK.

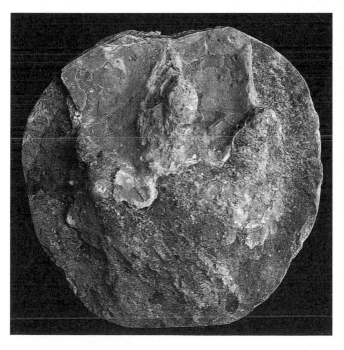

Skolithus

This is a bedding plane surface, which has the circular outlines of worm burrows upon it. The burrows have been filled by pale quartz sand, which contrasts with the darker quartzite surrounding them. This type of trace fossil is common in many rocks formed in intertidal environments, which is a typical place to find burrowing marine worms today.

Size The burrows are about 8mm (0.32in) in diameter.

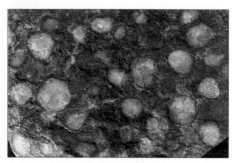

Distribution The specimen illustrated is from Cambrian rocks in northern Scotland.

Scolicia

This elongated, curving trace fossil represents the grazing trail of a gastropod mollusc. It is preserved here as a positive feature, which has infilled the groove left in the sandy sea-bed by the snail.

Size The field of view is about 200mm (8in).

Distribution Such fossils are common in rocks of many ages, from Palaeozoic to Recent. The example illustrated is from the Upper Carboniferous of West Yorkshire, UK.

Rotularia

These rounded fossils, commonly removed from the sediment that contained them, and appearing rather like flattened snail shells, are the burrows of polychaete worms. They are composed of calcium carbonate secreted by the worm to strengthen its burrow.

Size The burrows are about 15mm (0.6in) in diameter.
Distribution The specimens illustrated are from rocks of Eocene age in Sussex, UK.

Lithophaga burrows
and polychaete worm burrows

The specimen illustrated shows an inconformity, with pale Jurassic strata overlying darker Carboniferous rocks. The rounded burrows are those of the small bivalve mollusc *Lithophaga*, and the thinner burrows are those of polychaete worms.

Size The field of view is 200mm (8in) across.

Distribution This specimen is from the Mendip Hills of Somerset, UK. Similar burrowed surfaces are common in many parts of the fossil record.

Imbrichnus

These sinuous markings with many ridges across them are the
burrows made by a small mollusc, which worked its way
through the soft, muddy sediment on the sea-bed.
Size The specimen illustrated is 140mm (5.6in) across.
Distribution This example is from Upper Jurassic rocks in
southern England.

Thalassinoides

The specimen illustrated shows a bedding plane covered with
the joined and Y-shaped burrows believed to have been made
by a crustacean. They were originally made in the soft sea-bed,
and this fossil is a positive cast of the burrows. The arthropod
Glyphea (see p. 89) has been found associated with these
burrows, and may have been responsible for this trace fossil.
Faecal pellets are sometimes found in these burrows.
Size The area of view is about 120mm (4.8in) across.
Distribution The specimen shown is from Middle Jurassic
strata of Cleveland, UK. Such burrows are very common in
Jurassic rocks worldwide.

Coprolite

This convincing fossil is a piece of excrement left by a turtle. Such fossils are important in giving palaeontologists information about the diet of creatures. The term coprolite is reserved for larger droppings; faecal pellets are smaller droppings deposited by molluscs and arthropods.

Size The example illustrated is 30mm (1.2in) long and is covered with the iron mineral limonite. Coprolites can be well over 400mm (16in) long.

Distribution Such fossils are common throughout the fossil record worldwide. The specimen shown is from strata of Eocene age in North America.

Cruziana

These parallel marks are the trails left by trilobites, probably when they were feeding. There are many different types of *Cruziana*, some of which are interpreted as resting places and others as marks left by the creature's limbs.

Size The specimen illustrated is 140mm (5.6in) long.

Distribution The example shown is from Ordovician rocks at Rennes, France. These trace fossils are known from rocks of Palaeozoic age worldwide.

Acknowledgments

Many people have helped me with various aspects of the work that has gone into this book. Geological and other advice has always been forthcoming from Dr Hugh Torrens, of the University of Keele, UK, who made available specimens from his own collection for study and photography, and has always been able to answer my questions. The breadth and depth of his knowledge on all manner of subjects never ceases to amaze me. Ken Sedman, Cleveland County Geologist, gave me access to the fine collections and reference library in his care. I have photographed specimens in the National Museum of Wales in Cardiff, where Bob Owens organized a fine trilobite collection for me, and Ian Rolfe made fossil fishes and plants available at the Royal Museum of Scotland in Edinburgh. Jim Nunney allowed me to photograph the excellent collections in Leeds City Museum. Access to specimens in The City Museum, Stoke-on-Trent, was provided by Don Steward. Other people who have allowed me to photograph their collections include Jeff Mullroy, whose great enthusiasm for palaeontology has produced a wonderful, expertly curated collection, Sid Weatherill (of Hildoceras, Whitby), John Fraser of Leeds, Mike Marshall (of Terra Fauna, Whitby), and Lisa Crone of Middlesbrough.

Without the constant encouragement and untiring help of my wife, Helen, deadlines would never have been met and work never completed. She has a meticulous eye for detail when proof-reading, and has provided the index with her usual skill. Her help in cataloguing shots during photographic sessions not only saves time, but also means we have a set of captions that can be read! My three children have helped in a variety of ways. Daniel understands my word processor far better than I. Adam provides relaxation from writing by encouraging me to play cricket and football with him, and Emily banishes my worries with her guitar playing.

RSNC

The Royal Society for Nature Conservation is pleased to endorse these excellent, fully illustrated pocket guide books which provide invaluable information on the wildlife of Britain and Europe. Royalties from each book sold will go to help the RSNC's network of 48 Wildlife Trusts and over 50 Urban Wildlife Groups, all working to protect rare and endangered wildlife and threatened habitats. The RSNC and the Wildlife Trusts have a combined membership of 184,000 and look after over 1800 nature reserves. If you would like to find out more, please contact RSNC, The Green, Whitham Park, Lincoln LN5 7NR. Telephone 0522 752326.

Glossary

Aboral The surface of the test of an echinoid which contains the periproct and anus. Usually the upper surface.

Ambulacra (sing. **Ambulacrum**) Plates on the test of an echinoid which, in the regular echinoids, run in narrow bands around the test from periproct to peristome. In the irregular echinoids these bands may be petal-shaped and atrophied.

Ammonite An extinct group of molluscs, usually with a coiled shell.

Anterior The direction which is to the front of an organism.

Anthozoa A class of organisms including corals and sea-anemones.

Apical system A group of plates surrounding the anus of an echinoid.

Aptychus A curved structure, resembling a bivalve mollusc shell, which is believed to be part of the jaw apparatus of an ammonoid.

Arthropoda The phylum which contains numerous organisms characterised by a segmented exoskeleton. It includes the extinct trilobites. Among the modern representatives are the insects, crabs and lobsters.

Bedding plane The surface on which sediment is deposited, and which is preserved as a planar structure within a sedimentary rock.

Benthonic On the sea-bed.

Bifurcate To split in two, as for example the ribs on the shell of an ammonite where they cross the ventral surface.

Biserial Describing a graptolite stipe with thecae on both sides.

Bivalvia A class of molluscs including clams, oysters and tellins.

Boss A small protrusion on the test of an echinoid to which a spine is attached.

Brackish Describing water which is neither fresh nor salt, as when a river brings fresh water into an estuary.

Brachiopoda A phylum of marine, two-shelled organisms, which superficially resemble molluscs but have many very important biological differences.

Byssus A thin thread-like material by which some molluscs anchor themselves to the sea-bed.

Calcite A soft, easily broken mineral composed of calcium carbonate which makes up much limestone. Calcite is formed both organically, as in shells, and inorganically.

Calyx A cup in which an organism may live, as for example on the upper surface of a coral.

Cambrian A time period in the Palaeozoic era which lasted from 600 to 500 million years ago. It is named after Wales where it was first described.

Carapace An exoskeleton or dorsal shell.

Carboniferous A time period in the Palaeozoic era which lasted from 345 to 280 million years ago. The strata of this period contain much coal.

Carbonization A fossil-forming process where only the original carbon in the organism remains.

Cephalon The head-shield of an arthropod, for example in a trilobite.

Cephalopoda A class of mollusc characterized by a shell containing buoyancy chambers. This shell is usually coiled in a plane spiral.

Chert A silica rock, the material for which may come from organic sources such as the spicules of sponges.

Cirri Minute prehensile branches on the stems of crinoids.

Concretion A rounded lump of rock found in a sediment, often containing a fossil.

Columella The axis inside a gastropod shell.

Coprolite Fossilized dung.

Corallite An individual coral. It may remain solitary or be joined in a colony.

Cretaceous A time period which lasted from 136 to 65 million years ago. It is named after 'creta', the Greek word for chalk.

Crinoidea A class in the phylum Echinodermata, characterized by a stem and calyx with arms.

Denticulate Having a toothed or notched appearance.

Devonian A time period which lasted from 395 to 345 million years ago. It is named after Devon in SW England.

Dimorphism The occurrence, especially in fossils, of two distinct forms of a single species. These are usually interpreted as males and females.

Dissepiments A mass of small calcareous plates which thickens the wall of a corallite.

Dorsal The inner surface of the whorl of an ammonoid.

Echinodermata The phylum which contains such creatures as echinoids, crinoids and asteroids.

Eocene The part of the Tertiary period which lasted from 53.5 to 37.5 million years ago.

Era A large unit of geological time containing a number of periods.

Eurypterid A type of arthropod which was not unlike a scorpion and grew to large size.

Evolute Describing loose coiling of a cephalopod shell, where the whorls do not obscure one another.

Exoskeleton An outside or external skeleton.

Flint A type of chert found in nodules and bands in the Cretaceous chalk of Western Europe. It is formed of microcrystalline silica.

Foramen An opening near or at the beak of a brachiopod shell.

Gastropoda A class of mollusc many members of which are characterized by a spirally-coiled shell. The class includes snails and slugs.

Genus (plural **Genera**) A group of very similar organisms which can be further subdivided into species. In the ammonite *Dactylioceras commune*, the word *Dactylioceras* is the generic (genus) name and *commune* the specific (species) name.

Glabella The central part of the head of a trilobite, probably where the centre of the nervous system was housed.

Goniatites A group of ammonoids which were abundant during the Devonian and Carboniferous periods.

Heterocercal Describing a fish tail which has the vertebral column in a larger upper lobe.

Hexacoral A type of coral which has its septa in groups of six.

Interglacial A time between ice advances during a prolonged ice-age.

Involute Describing tight coiling of a cephalopod shell where the outer whorls obscure the inner ones.

Keel A ridge running around the ventral surface of a cephalopod shell.

Lappet An extension protruding from the aperture of an ammonoid shell.

Leaching The movement of chemicals by water, often in a downward direction.

Macroconch The larger shell of a dimorphic pair. Especially used with species where there is a size difference.

Mesozoic An era of geological time containing the Triassic, Jurassic and Cretaceous periods.

Mica A silicate mineral characterized by its flaky appearance, bright lustre and low hardness.

Microconch The smaller of two shells in a dimorphic pair. The opposite of macroconch.

Miocene Part of the Tertiary period lasting from 22.5 to 5 million years ago.

Mollusca A large phylum which contains cephalopods, bivalves and gastropods.

Myrapod A small terrestrial arthropod.

Nema A thin thread at the end of a graptolite's stipe.

Nodule A rounded lump of rock, often only a few centimetres in diameter, occurring in a sedimentary rock. Nodules of ironstone and calcite often develop in shales and clays. Perfect fossils may be found in these structures.

Oolith A small (about 2mm) grain of sediment of calcareous composition, with a concentric layered structure. These grains make oolitic limestone.

Operculum A shell which acts as a lid.

Orthocone Describing a straight cephalopod shell.

Ossicle A single plate from the stem of a crinoid.

Palaeocene The part of the Tertiary period which lasted from 65 to 53.5 million years ago.

Palaeozoic The era containing the Cambrian, Ordovician, Silurian, Devonian, Carboniferous and Permian periods. It is usually divided into upper and lower, with three periods in each division.

Pedicle valve The larger of the two valves in a brachiopod shell, which contains the pedicle opening.

Period A unit of geological time. Periods are generally of less than 100 million years' duration. A number of periods make up an era.

Periproct The flexible arrangement of small plates within the apical system surrounding an echinoid's anus.

Peristome The group of plates surrounding an echinoid's mouth.

Permian The time period which lasted from 280 to 225 million years ago.

Pinnate Describing a leaf consisting of leaflets arranged on either side of a central stem.

Planktonic Near the surface of the sea.

Pleistocene The earlier part of the Quaternary era, lasting from 2 to 0.1 million years ago and characterized by widespread glaciation.

Polyp A soft organism with a flexible body, as in a coral or sea anemone.

Porifera The phylum containing the sponges.

Posterior The direction towards the rear of an organism.

Pre-Cambrian The part of geological time before 600 million years ago.

Protoconch The initial small part of a shell. In the cephalopods this is in the very centre.

Punctation Pits on the surface of a shell.

Pygidium The tail segments of an arthropod's exoskeleton.

Saline Having a high concentration of salt.

Septum (plural **Septa**) Internal partition which separates the chambers in a mollusc shell or a coral.

Silurian The period of time which lasted from 440 to 395 million years ago.

Siphon A soft tube which extends from the body of a mollusc, especially in the bivalves, outside the shell margin.

Siphuncle A thin tube running from the body to the innermost coil of the shell, passing through the septa, in a cephalopod mollusc. Its position varies: in nautiloids it tends to be in a central position through each septum but in ammonoids (with the exception of the Clymeniida, where it is dorsal) it has a ventral position.

Spicules The skeletal parts of a sponge. These can be calcareous or siliceous.

Strata (singular **Stratum**) Layers or beds of sedimentary rock.

Stipe The long part of a graptolite structure on which the thecae are situated.

Suture A line of joining. The cephalopods have suture lines where the internal septa meet and join the inner surface of the shell wall. These vary in their complexity in the different groups of this class.

System The rocks deposited during a geological period. The Jurassic system is the various rock strata deposited during the Jurassic period.

Tabulae The horizontal divisions found in a coral.

Teleost A modern type of bony fish. These fish have a symmetrical tail and a skeleton covered with skin.

Tertiary The time period which lasted from 65 to 2 million years ago.

Test The skeleton of a creature, especially used of echinoids.

Thecae (singular **Theca**) The cup-like structures on, for example, a graptolite stipe.

Thorax The main body of an organism, especially used for the Arthropoda.

Trace fossil A fossil which is no part of the organism. It may be, for example, a footprint, a burrow, a coprolite or an egg.

Triassic The period of geological time which lasted from 225 to 190 million years ago.

Umbilicus The very centre of a coiled shell.

Umbo The beak-like part of a bivalve or brachiopod shell.

Uniserial Describing a graptolite stipe with thecae on only one side.

Vascular Having veins.

Venter The outer surface of the whorl of a cephalopod mollusc.

Ventral surface The underneath of an organism. The opposite of dorsal.

Whorl The coil of a shell, especially used of cephalopods.

Zone A small unit of geological time. A number of zones make up a period. In some parts of the time-scale zones are of about one million years or less in length. Each zone is named after an index fossil. This fossil is chosen because it occurs only during the time represented by the rocks of that zone.

Bibliography

This is not an exhaustive list, but is intended to widen the reader's knowledge and add to the information contained in this book. By consulting the bibliographies in the books listed below, the subject can be studied in even further detail.

Barthel, **K.W.**, **Swinburne**, **N.H.M.**, and **Conway Morris S.**, Solnhofen, a study in Mesozoic Palaeontology, Cambridge University Press, 1990.

British Museum (Natural History), British Caenozoic Fossils, London, 1982.

British Museum (Natural History), British Mesozoic Fossils, London 1982.

British Museum (Natural History), British Palaeozoic Fossils, London, 1982.

Clarkson, **E.K.M.**, Invertebrate Palaeontology and Evolution, Allen and Unwin, London, 1979.

Halstead, **L.B.**, Evolution of Mammals, Lowe, London, 1978.

Halstead, **L.B.**, Hunting the Past, Hamish Hamilton, London, 1982.

McKerrow, **W.S.**, The Ecology of Fossils, Duckworth, London, 1978.

Miles, **R.S.**, Palaeozoic Fishes, Chapman Hall, London, 1971.

Moore, **R.C.**, Treatise on Invertebrate Palaeontology, University of Kansas, 1953 onwards.

Morton, **J.E.**, Molluscs, Hutchinson, London, 1967.

Norman, **D.**, Illustrated Encyclopedia of Dinosaurs, Salamander, London, 1985.

Pellant, **C.**, Earthscope, Salamander, London, 1985.

Pellant, **C.**, Rocks, Minerals and Fossils of the World, Pan, London, 1990.

Romer, **A.S.**, Vertebrate Palaeontology, University of Chicago Press, 1966.

Rudwick, **M.J.S.**, Living and Fossil Brachiopods, Hutchinson, London, 1970.

Tucker Abbott, **R.**, Seashells of the Northern Hemisphere, Dragon's World, London, 1990.

There are a number of journals published by the various geological and palaeontological societies. Membership of these societies is of value to those who make an in depth study of the subject, or who are professional geologists. This is not to say, however, that amateurs are not welcomed, and indeed, the body of palaeontological knowledge is frequently added to by amateurs. One journal, however, which is far less obscure than most, and which certainly caters for the amateur as well as the professional, is Geology Today, published by Blackwell Scientific Publications, Oxford, UK. This frequently covers topics of palaeontological interest.

Index

Bold type indicates main entries